THE PUBLIC LIBRARY AND THE CITY

A Publication of the Joint Center for Urban Studies of the Massachusetts Institute of Technology and Harvard University

This book is one of a series published under the auspices of the Joint Center for Urban Studies, a cooperative venture of the Massachusetts Institute of Technology and Harvard University. The Joint Center was founded in 1959 to organize and encourage research on urban and regional problems. Participants have included scholars from the fields of anthropology, architecture, business, city planning, economics, education, engineering, history, law, philosophy, political science, and sociology.

The findings and conclusions of this book are, as with all Joint Center publications, solely the responsibility of the contributors.

Other books published in the Joint Center series include:

CHARLES ABRAMS, *Man's Struggle for Shelter in an Urbanizing World.* The M.I.T. Press, 1964.

WILLIAM ALONSO, *Location and Land Use.* Harvard University Press, 1964.

MARTIN ANDERSON, *The Federal Bulldozer.* The M.I.T. Press, 1964.

DONALD APPLEYARD, KEVIN LYNCH, and JOHN R. MYER, *The View from the Road.* The M.I.T. Press, 1964.

EDWARD C. BANFIELD and JAMES Q. WILSON, *City Politics.* Harvard University Press and the M.I.T. Press, 1963.

JOHN E. BURCHARD and OSCAR HANDLIN, editors, *The Historian and the City.* The M.I.T. Press, 1963.

BERNARD J. FRIEDEN, *The Future of Old Neighborhoods.* The M.I.T. Press, 1964.

NATHAN GLAZER and DANIEL MOYNIHAN, *Beyond the Melting Pot.* The M.I.T. Press, 1963.

CHARLES HAAR, *Law and Land: Anglo-American Planning Practice.* Harvard University Press, 1964.

KEVIN LYNCH, *The Image of the City.* The M.I.T. Press, 1960.

LLOYD RODWIN, *Housing and Economic Progress.* The M.I.T. Press, 1961.

STEPHAN THERNSTROM, *Poverty and Progress.* Harvard University Press, 1964.

SAM B. WARNER, JR., *Streetcar Suburbs.* Harvard University Press, 1962.

MORTON AND LUCIA WHITE, *The Intellectual Versus the City: From Thomas Jefferson to Frank Lloyd Wright.* Harvard University Press, 1962.

RALPH W. CONANT, *editor*

THE PUBLIC LIBRARY AND THE CITY

THE M.I.T. PRESS
MASSACHUSETTS INSTITUTE OF TECHNOLOGY
CAMBRIDGE, MASSACHUSETTS, AND LONDON, ENGLAND

Second Printing, April 1966

Library of Congress Catalog Number 65-27504
Printed in the United States of America

ISBN 0-262-53219-0 (paperback)

ACKNOWLEDGMENTS

The Symposium on Library Functions in the Changing Metropolis out of which this book grew was sponsored by the National Book Committee with funds from the Council on Library Resources and the Joint Center for Urban Studies of M.I.T. and Harvard. Dan Lacy, Managing Director of the American Book Publishers Council, and Martin Meyerson, former director of the Joint Center, were largely responsible for conceiving the symposium. Margaret W. Dudley, former executive secretary of the National Book Committee, contributed generously of time and talent in the planning and execution of the symposium.

Emerson Greenaway, Oscar Handlin, Everett C. Hughes, Norton Long, John G. Lorenz, Virginia H. Mathews, Kathleen Molz, Frederick Wagman, and James Q. Wilson were among those who read the edited papers and helped shape the volume.

SYMPOSIUM ON LIBRARY FUNCTIONS IN THE CHANGING METROPOLIS

Endicott House
Dedham, Massachusetts
May 1963

Contributors to this Volume

EDWARD C. BANFIELD *Professor of Urban Government, Harvard University*

HOWARD S. BECKER *Research Associate, Institute for the Study of Human Problems, Stanford University*

RALPH BLASINGAME, JR. *Associate Professor, Graduate School of Library Service, Rutgers—The State University*

JOHN E. BURCHARD *Dean Emeritus, School of Humanities and Social Science, Massachusetts Institute of Technology*

RALPH W. CONANT *Assistant to the Director, Joint Center for Urban Studies of the Massachusetts Institute of Technology and Harvard University*

JEROME CUSHMAN *Librarian, New Orleans Public Library*

ALLISON DAVIS *Professor of Education, University of Chicago*

PHILIP H. ENNIS *Assistant Professor, Graduate Library School, University of Chicago*

HERBERT J. GANS *Associate Professor of Sociology and Education, Teachers College, Columbia University*

NATHAN GLAZER *Professor of Sociology, University of California at Berkeley*

EMERSON GREENAWAY *Director, Free Library of Philadelphia*

LEONARD GRUNDT *Graduate School of Library Service, Rutgers—The State University*

WILLIAM F. HELLMUTH *Dean and Professor of Economics, Oberlin College*

DAN LACY *Managing Director, American Book Publishers Council*

RICHARD L. MEIER *Research Social Scientist, Mental Health Research Institute, University of Michigan*

ROBERT H. SALISBURY *Associate Professor of Political Science, Washington University*

CHARLES M. TIEBOUT *Professor of Economics, University of Washington*

ROBERT J. WILLIS *Department of Economics, University of Washington*

Other Participants

EVERETT C. HUGHES, *Chairman of the symposium, Professor of Sociology, Brandeis University*

BERNARD BERELSON *Vice President, The Population Council*

CLARA E. BREED *City Librarian, San Diego Public Library*

JAMES E. BRYAN *Director, The Public Library of Newark*

HENRY C. CAMPBELL *Chief Librarian, Toronto Public Library*

EDWIN CASTAGNA *Director, Enoch Pratt Free Library, Baltimore*

KATHARINE G. CLARK *Assistant to the Director, Joint Center for Urban Studies of the Massachusetts Institute of Technology and Harvard University*

LOUIS G. COWAN *Director, Morse Communication Research Center, Brandeis University*

MARGARET W. DUDLEY *Executive Secretary, National Book Committee*

JOHN T. EASTLICK *Librarian, Denver Public Library*

JASON EPSTEIN *Vice President, Random House, Inc.*

MRS. GEORGE J. GALICK *Director, Division of Library Extension, Commonwealth of Massachusetts*

W. J. J. GORDON *Chairman of the Board, Synectics, Inc.*

ROBERT GUTMAN *Urban Studies Center, Rutgers—The State University*

JAN HAJDA *Professor of Social Relations, Johns Hopkins University*

OSCAR HANDLIN *Winthrop Professor of History, Harvard University*

THE REV. G. DANIEL LITTLE *Associate for Urban Ministries, Division of Church Strategy and Development, Board of National Missions of the United Presbyterian Church in the U.S.A.*

WILLIAM N. LOCKE *Director of Libraries, Massachusetts Institute of Technology*

MILTON E. LORD *Director, Boston Public Library*

JOHN G. LORENZ *Director, Division of Library Services, U.S. Office of Education*

JULIUS MARGOLIS *Professor of Economics, Stanford University*

DONALD G. MARQUIS *Professor of Industrial Management, Massachusetts Institute of Technology*

VIRGINIA H. MATHEWS *National Book Committee*

MARTIN MEYERSON *Dean, College of Environmental Design, University of California at Berkeley*

ERNEST I. MILLER *Librarian, Public Library of Cincinnati and Hamilton County*

KATHLEEN MOLZ *Editor,* Wilson Library Bulletin

KATHERINE MURPHY *Librarian, The Rotch Library, Massachusetts Institute of Technology*

TALCOTT PARSONS *Professor of Sociology, Harvard University*

PHYLLIS A. REINHARDT *Librarian, Hillyer Art Library, Smith College*

FRANK RIESSMAN *Associate Professor of Psychiatry, Albert Einstein College of Medicine*

MELVILLE J. RUGGLES *Vice President, Council on Library Resources, Inc.*

HELEN R. SATTLEY *Director, School Library Service, City of New York*

HENRY B. SCHECHTER *Director, Division of Housing Analysis, Housing and Home Finance Agency*

CAROLINE SHILLABER *Librarian of the Graduate School of Design, Harvard University*

EDWARD F. SINTZ *Assistant Librarian, Kansas City Public Library*

SAMRAY SMITH *Editor,* ALA Bulletin

WILLIAM E. SPAULDING *Chairman of the Board, Houghton Mifflin Company*

FRANCIS R. ST. JOHN *President, Francis R. St. John Library Consultants, Inc.*

EDITH G. STULL *Associate Professor of Education, Hofstra University*

THEODORE WALLER *Vice President, Educational Divisions, Grolier, Inc.*

SAM B. WARNER, JR. *Assistant Professor of History and Architecture, Washington University*

THOMAS J. WILSON *Director, Harvard University Press*

ROBERT C. WOOD *Professor of Political Science, Massachusetts Institute of Technology*

CONTENTS

RALPH W. CONANT

INTRODUCTION

The public library in the United States is a community facility dedicated to a stanch tradition of "service to everyone." But this broad concept of service, though admirable, implies objectives librarians are increasingly hard put to meet with available resources. Thinly spread programs and services span education, information, culture, and recreation. Library administrators stretch meager budgets to anticipate and respond to an extraordinary diversity of requirements thrust upon the library by a constantly shifting clientele. Public libraries have done well — some even brilliantly — in the face of drastic change; but creative new responses are needed to cope with the scale and character of the problems at hand.

This volume is an edited collection of some papers from the 1963 Symposium on Library Functions in the Changing Metropolis sponsored by the Joint Center for Urban Studies and the National Book Committee. Not all the papers delivered at the Symposium are included, and papers by Banfield, Blasingame, and myself were written especially for this volume. The authors are urban social scientists, economists, historians, sociologists, political scientists, planners, communication experts, library scholars, and library administrators. The papers are about libraries and cities, and their main purpose is to raise issues about the character of cities and the future of libraries whose milieu is the city.

Some of the issues confronting public libraries are these:

How will urban libraries be affected by social, political, and economic changes in the city? How should libraries respond to these changes? What new responsibilities should libraries accept in contributing to the direction of change?

How far should the public library go toward developing high-level reference services and research resources required by sophisticated new urban industrial complexes?

The larger and more complicated cities grow the harder it is to get accurate information about them. Free telephone reference service, largely for business and industry, has become a considerable task for metropolitan libraries. Should public libraries continue with this responsibility or should other specialized new institutions take over this critical function?

How shall public libraries retain traditional leadership in the high culture of the community and how shall they develop new methods of contributing to the dissemination of culture in expanding city regions?

Traditionally libraries have been a refuge for students, who use them for study, research, meetings with friends, reading for recreation. In recent years students have become the chief users of libraries, and librarians fear their sheer numbers are crowding out adults. What division of labor should be worked out between libraries and schools to meet the needs of students and preserve library resources for other functions?

Libraries have also been one of the places where the talented of the lower classes have learned middle-class values. What role should the public library play in acculturation and education of low-income groups who suffer economic deprivation because of functional illiteracy?

Spatial dispersion of library facilities may be a tempting way of dealing with the demand of outward moving middle-class clients of the library. Will the great central institution gradually be dismantled and even abandoned in favor of smaller, more accessible units? One answer falls between the extremes: New technologies may make it possible to maintain and expand central facilities as a reservoir of resources that can be made available to branches.

The papers and commentaries published here deal intimately with problems of cities and with issues facing public libraries.

Philip Ennis leads off the set of essays about the diverse urban groups we call library consumers and library nonconsumers. Ennis, a sociologist at the University of Chicago Graduate Library School, writes factually about readers and nonreaders. He argues, from evidence about reading trends and library use, that libraries have a bigger potential audience than they did a decade ago — but the audience is harder to reach. Ennis reviews demographic and cultural changes that could affect the level and intensity of reading in the potential reading publics. He re-examines the statistics on who reads what and how much. The librarian, Ennis asserts, has a stake in book reading, and his role is bound to make a decisive difference in what happens to book reading in the future. At present, he charges, libraries are "merely responding to public demands and to the trends of the publishers." What should they be doing? First, re-examine traditional goals, assign priorities, and move energetically on the priority objectives. Ennis stops short of suggesting priorities, but he cautions against setting unrealistic and unattainable goals.

Allison Davis and Howard Becker write vivid analyses of problems of lower-class youth. Becker asks these questions: What does it mean to grow up in our society? What happens after high school, in the years when boys and girls become men and women? How does a person learn the things he needs to know and acquire the skills he needs to become a mature adult? Professor Davis focuses on the cultural perspectives of lower-class people and on the relative importance of cognitive and emotional needs in their lives. His message to the librarian is straightforward: "To begin to solve the problem of attracting low-income people to libraries, one must understand the culture and the basic way of life of the lower class, and how this culture differs from that of middle-class people." Becker is skeptical about the role of libraries as effective agents in the maturing process and education of lower-class youth: "This is one of a perhaps large class of problems which require for their solution kinds of action for which the library is not equipped and which might best be left to other institutions better able to handle them."

Functions of public libraries are explored in a provocative set of essays by a group of scholars whose thoughtful insights reflect a genuine interest in the future character of the urban library institutions.

Herbert Gans urges development of a public library system in city regions. He would combine the neighborhood concept of the library with the principle, suggested also by Lacy, that libraries ought to cater to people not served by other methods of book distribution. Libraries would be planned for the kinds of people who live in its service areas: in middle-class neighborhoods the contemporary library is suitable; in low-income areas, a library is needed that invites rather than rejects the poorly educated person. Moreover, libraries should teach reading to adult illiterates. Providing for diverse demands is, in Gans' view, central to the planning of the future metropolitan library system. "This approach to library planning is based on the idea that existing institutions not only should perform effectively their original functions but also should be adapted to the changing needs of their communities."

Nathan Glazer speaks for the old-fashioned view of the library, the one made of granite, to which he retreated from the city neighborhood of his childhood. Glazer's view goes far deeper than personal nostalgia. He suggests the timeless, ancient, permanent functions of the library, the features worth preserving in the rush of contemporary change: the repository of the records of civilization, the institution of social mobility for ambitious youth, the refuge for the bookworm and the browser, the place "to be alone in a productive and restorative way," a center of information, an accent point in the contemporary urban texture of unending and unvarying forms. The role of the library in the city is for Glazer "something special and distinctive, creating a unique quality . . . one that we cannot afford to lose."

Richard Meier speculates on the communications functions of the urban public library in the more general context of the increasingly complex communication requirements of metropolitan society. In Meier's vision of communication in the future metropolis, the extraordinarily difficult task of sorting out and retaining reusable information and materials must be divided between the library and two highly specialized new institutions: the data bank and the documentation center. Regional data banks now coming into fashion in several areas will collect retrievable information about the workings of urban services. Most data banks will be public facilities established to assemble trend data for local and regional public decision making. Documentation centers will assemble new materials in science, technology, and literature from the world at large. These two mechanized compilations of information will draw heavily from each other when responding to complex questions. "But there is much information that is valuable, yet inconvenient to store and retrieve by mechanical means." Here is where the metropolitan library comes into the picture. "In the future we may expect that the routine and high-volume demands now made upon a library would gradually be divested from it, while the unique services to adult education and scholarship would be expanded."

Meier avoids the pitfalls of spelling out the troublesome details of the proposed division of labor. He does not concern himself with administrative arrangements that would ensure coordination in such crucial matters as which institution handles what materials.

Charles Tiebout and Robert J. Willis examine the economic rationale of free public libraries and challenge familiar criticisms that the principal defect in metropolitan library service is the scattering of small facilities among dozens of separate municipalities. They deny that any inadequacy in metropolitan library services is attributable to faulty government organization. From their point of view the nut of the problem is that the user is not asked to pay his share; if he were charged the price he is willing to pay for benefits received, revenues would cover the cost of improved services up to a level where further improvements would not attract further users. The functions of libraries would thus be determined by the market demand for services. Services not wanted would find no buyers.

Edward C. Banfield argues that the public library no longer serves its original purpose as a means to encourage assimilation of working-class immigrants to the middle-class style of life. Immigrants are now fully assimilated, and income levels are high enough to allow private consumption. The present-day poor do not use the public library partly because they lack motivation for self-improvement and partly because libraries are middle-class institutions that do not appeal to the poor or reject them.

If the problem of the poor *is* assimilation, one must start with very young children. This is a job for the schools, not libraries. "Something much more fundamental than library service may be needed — for example, compulsory nursery school attendance from the age of two or three." The public library should not be a substitute for the school library. "In fairness to both the children and the adults, the schools ought to have adequate libraries of their own."

Demands of fiction readers should be met by private rental libraries and paperback stores, not public libraries. The public library should confine its service to the "serious" reader. (Banfield defines serious reading as any which improves one's stock of knowledge, enlarges one's horizons, or improves one's values.) The service to these readers should be far better than most libraries now provide, and to make sure it is better it should be placed on a fee basis. Services provided for a fee might include: home delivery of books, microfilm copy service, quick and easy interlibrary loans, soundproof cubicles on a monthly rental basis, annotated bibliographies and specialized reading lists, tutorial assistance, mail-order counter with catalogues of all publishers.

Writing from wide experience as both publisher and librarian, Dan Lacy urges that libraries assume active responsibility for expressing demand and providing channels of distribution for materials needed by "segments of society not now effectively literate." Lacy explains that dissemination of print through private publishers is effectively confined to middle and upper segments of the socio-economic-educational pyramid because "only there does a demand exist that is adequate to sustain the machinery of distribution." He concludes that a failure on the part of libraries to discharge this responsibility could "contribute one more element to already potentially explosive social situation."

Jerome Cushman reviews current issues of public libraries as seen by an experienced librarian. Cushman is idealistic about library goals; practical about probability of achievement. He offers no easy solutions, no innovations. For Cushman the primary task of the public library is education. The library, he asserts, "must satisfy more than a recreational or reference need in order to discharge its responsibility." He says the basic concern of the library profession is "a traumatic encounter with . . . school population, from junior high through the university." Books and periodicals are wearing out. . . .

Adults are being discouraged from using the public library. The search for a solution has yielded no answer and librarians are beginning to feel guilty about their inability to meet the demands of students and still attract adult clientele. They want to give good service and they want to welcome young people "and help them reach their educational potentialities," but, Cushman warns, they are not up to the task . . . . they are not up to the requirements of study space, multiple copy demands for books and reference materials, reference service.

Cushman offers brief descriptions of other matters which librarians believe are the concern of public libraries: the nonreader ("We need to find ways of making reading more meaningful for more people"); cultural deprivation ("Specialized services [need to be] offered . . . to provide an adequate . . . educational experience for many who cannot fit into the regular library usage framework"); adult education ("There is a leveling off in public library activities in this field since the Fund for Adult Education ceased its activities [but] . . . new and more extensive methods should be developed to make it possible for the library to add creative depth to its service"); the book collection ("[It] must expand in order to meet a new emphasis on specialization, research, and changing fields of knowledge"); documentation ("The necessity of using scientific facilities to communicate knowledge across barriers of time, space, and language has come with startling rapidity"). Librarians are also concerned with the problems of the foreign-born reader with language and acculturation problems; professional staff training and recruitment of future library technicians and administrators; and with problems of interlibrary cooperation, especially in metropolitan areas where political boundary lines may be serious barriers to optimum library service. As things stand, public libraries in most metropolitan regions are hard put to plan, budget, and program on an area-wide basis.

Robert Salisbury and William Hellmuth, in papers on the changing structure of cities, provide detailed accounts of salient trends in urban politics and economics. Their essays set the practical framework and projections that library directors need in order to maintain perspective on extremely complex environments. Salisbury reviews familiar facts of core city population decline in the 1950–1960 census period and the concurrent growth of suburbs; the increasing proportions of low-income population in core cities, shrinking tax base, demoralization of public education, disintegration of physical plant, and gradual loss of effective political leadership. The new immigrants are not effectively mobilized by the old political machines. "Organization politics is a feeble shadow of the past." Yet in the decay of party leadership "we are witnessing a reconvergence of political and economic power." Civic notables who see their central city investments threatened have generated "a heightened sense of involvement in . . . their community's economic and social well-being." Together with the "experts" in urban revitalization and the politicians, the economic leaders are striving to rebuild. What does this movement mean for public libraries? Library trustees are frequently close to the civic notables, so if they choose to exercise their influence, they could presumably help get a higher priority for libraries on the civic development agenda.

Moreover, professional librarians can have contacts with government agencies. Land clearance, housing, and welfare officials are examples of agencies out of which productive cooperative effort could develop. Salisbury observes, "Depending on how effectively the lines of communication with those who have power over community resource allocation are developed, the library will fare well or badly in the competition for public money."

Hellmuth warns about rising library expenditures and resulting pressures for increased revenues. Libraries, he thinks, have an advantage in this situation because their budgets are relatively small and are not a decisive factor in tax increases. But they do not have the emotional appeal, public contact and "visibility" of public schools. "Thus," Hellmuth concludes, "large expenditure increases, especially if they must be voted separately, may be difficult to achieve." Hellmuth believes libraries should fare well in the large metropolitan regions, "provided they offer efficient and high-quality service and cooperate on a broad basis with other public and private libraries in the metropolitan area."

Emerson Greenaway, director of the Free Library of Philadelphia, suggests a realistic look at the future of libraries in a review of several important trends in organization of library services: state and regional service systems, central resource libraries, realignment and redistribution of fiscal resources. In his special concern with the problem of students, Greenaway suggests at the close of his paper a division of labor between libraries and schools: have libraries for children's recreational reading, leaving to the schools the reference work and supply of curriculum-related materials; have student centers in public libraries to take care of high school and college materials and services; have adult collections for the graduate student, faculty, and postschool adult. In an epilogue written in February 1965, Greenaway summarizes the progress librarians have made in their drive for new federal funds in the Higher Education Facilities Act, the Library Services and Construction Act of 1964, and potentially in the Economic Opportunities Act of 1964, the Elementary and Secondary Education Act of 1965 and the Higher Education Act of 1965. Greenaway warns: "The problem facing librarians now becomes one of making the most effective and efficient use of federal funds . . . and keeping a balance between federal, state and local monies."

In the paper following Greenaway's, Ralph Blasingame and I outline some of the questions librarians need answered as a basis for shaping new policies and programs and as a basis for judging the relevance of traditional ones. The problem Greenaway and other library leaders face is to rethink the fundamental character and objectives of the institutions *from a fresh perspective*. This may only be possible if library leaders seek help outside the library world. This is not to say the social scientists have a monopoly on wisdom and research know-how. It is to say that the library profession is an extremely stable system whose norms and values are firmly established and whose tap root is very deep in social history. Such systems are hard to change from within partly because leaders feel threatened by new concepts and partly because the habits and training of operatives are costly and difficult to adapt.

Nonetheless, urban institutions that fail to tackle new problems are likely to miss exciting new opportunities. Likewise, institutions that fail to re-evaluate traditional objectives are in danger of becoming weighted down with outmoded programs that sap vitality, discourage able recruits, and repel public and private supporters.

Library administrators will be hard put to sponsor research that genuinely questions the relevance of traditional service and realistically appraises new opportunities. If innovation in library service is required, the inquiry behind the innovation must be the work of detached observers. Yet the invitation to innovation must come from inside the profession.

John Burchard's pungent critique of the Symposium is a wise reminder that a single short conference may be too awkward a way to begin the difficult process of thinking through the shaping and reshaping of urban libraries.

The public librarians on the firing line are nearly desperate for solutions to immediate practical problems. They also sense the urgency of sketching a design for an uncertain future. They sought in the Symposium answers to immediate problems and they hoped for clues to the future. They got little satisfaction on either score, but they made a beginning toward a broadened view of the city regions in which they will create new concepts of service. They may not again use the device of a brief conference for trying to solve tough issues, but hopefully they will continue to draw on the resources of scholars who are pioneering in research on cities.

PART I

CONSUMERS AND NONCONSUMERS

PHILIP H. ENNIS

*THE LIBRARY CONSUMER**

Readers and Nonreaders

The first part of this paper introduces evidence about what is happening to reading and to libraries in the context of demographic and cultural changes of the past fifteen years. The burden of my argument is that the library has a bigger potential audience than it did a decade ago, but this audience is harder to reach. This is a useful time period, not only because of the decade-marking census, but also because it was in 1948 that the Public Library Inquiry surveyed the library situation. Since that time television has saturated the country, reaching about 90 per cent of American households;[1] paperback books, both quality and mass circulation, have made decisive changes in the reading landscape; and the demographic and educational changes in the American population have altered the social base for reading.

In the July 1961 issue of *Library Trends,* Philip Hauser and Martin Taitel presented a mass of census statistics relevant to libraries.[2] Three demographic changes between 1950 and 1960 are most important. The first is the increase of those known to be most likely to read — students and the well educated. Although the population

* I am indebted to my colleagues Leon Carnovsky and Herman Fussler for critical readings of an earlier draft of this paper. I did not always follow their advice, however.

1 Gary A. Steiner, *The People Look at Television: A Study of Audience Attitudes* (New York: Alfred A. Knopf, Inc., 1963), p. 17.

2 Philip M. Hauser and Martin Taitel, "Population Trends — Prologue to Library Development," *Library Trends,* Vol. 10 (July 1961), pp. 10–67.

grew by only 18 per cent, those enrolled in school (ranging in age from five to thirty-four years old) increased by 53 per cent.[3] In 1950 there were slightly over 38 million people who were high school graduates, 37 per cent of the adult population. By 1960 high school graduates had increased to almost 52 million, or 45 per cent of the adult population. This is a 35 per cent increase. Similarly, the proportion of college graduates in the population increased by 34 per cent over the decade.[4]

I have no statistics measuring the exact amount of educational activity in the United States or its change over the decade, but I am sure it has far greater scope than has been indicated here. In his national inventory of adult education for the Carnegie Corporation, John Johnstone of the National Opinion Research Center reports that at least one out of five adults was engaged sometime in the year 1961–1962 in some kind of organized or independent study.[5] This might be in the tremendous enterprise of industrial training programs, in extension or other adult courses, or in the educational programs of voluntary associations.

I do not know how many of these programs develop book readers in the ordinary sense of the word, but it is almost certain that these adult students are reading something. Information regarding types and sources of their reading materials would be valuable, but I am not sure this will be forthcoming from the NORC study.

Another demographic change of significance for the public library is the growing number of older people. The number of people over sixty-five years old increased almost twice as fast as the population as a whole, that is, almost 35 per cent between 1950 and 1960.[6] Reading declines with age, but there are definite pressures for libraries to create special services and programs for the aged. This enlarged group of older people, mainly a potential rather than an actual audience for the library, creates a problem of allocation of library resources.

[3] *Ibid.*, Table 18, p. 59.

[4] *Ibid.*, Table 24, p. 64.

[5] John W. C. Johnstone, *Volunteers for Learning: A Study of the Educational Pursuits of American Adults* (Chicago: National Opinion Research Center, University of Chicago, February 1963), Report No. 89, p. 25.

[6] Hauser, *op. cit.*, Table 15, p. 57.

The third major type of population change important to the library is the geographical reshuffling of the population. According to the figures of Hauser and Taitel, the Standard Metropolitan Statistical Areas — central cities of over 50,000 plus their surrounding "metropolitan" areas — grew faster than did smaller cities and the countryside. Between 1950 and 1960 the SMSA's increased in population 25 per cent, compared with a 6 per cent increase in the rest of the country. The most significant part of this continuing urbanization is the difference in the growth of the central parts of the metropolitan area and its outlying suburbs. The central cities of the Standard Metropolitan Areas grew in population by 9.4 per cent while outlying areas grew by 47.7 per cent.[7] Three major problems for the libraries arise from this high speed development of suburbs.

The first is that the library will try to follow its patrons by building branches and getting bookmobiles to the areas where the population has moved, since it has been shown repeatedly that use of the library is closely related to distance from library facilities. However, this is expensive in terms of capital outlay, duplicate purchasing, and staffing. Moreover, the quality of a collection at a small branch simply cannot match that of a centralized and specialized collection. The librarian must make a crucial decision: should he develop his central library's collection and services, or should he try to expand outward to meet the needs of a physically dispersed and dispersing clientele? Perhaps some day technological innovation can let him do both by greatly facilitating central storage and processing while maximizing dispersion of the collection to where the patrons are. Such developments are likely to be expensive and in any case are not on the immediate horizon.

The second aspect of the decentralization of the metropolitan city is that the outlying suburbs have become fragmented into autonomous localities, each with its own laws and traditions. The result is that it is practically impossible to create larger library districts to consolidate resources. The proliferation of small, inadequate libraries around the city forces the demand for books to express itself through channels other than the public library.

7 Hauser, *op. cit.*, Table 7, p. 50.

Third, because of patterns of residential restrictions and low economic power, ethnic minorities, particularly Negro and Spanish-speaking groups, have been slowest to move from the center of the city. These groups are hungry for education. Guy Garrison has repeatedly shown that the greatest support for library bond referenda comes from those areas with the highest educational background and from those areas with high Negro populations.[8] Studies now carried on by the Social Psychology Laboratory of the University of Chicago under the direction of Fred Strodtbeck confirm a hunger for education among Negroes. But they show a poignant paradox: Negro mothers greatly wish to have their children advance in school, but are often ill-equipped to help them. They either do the wrong things (which can kill the already fragile motivation to learn) or they haven't the skills and facilities to do the right thing. One of these "right things," Strodtbeck feels, is to read books to the children. Here is a tremendous task for the urban library in predominantly Negro areas: to create programs that will take books out of the library and get them into the hands of mothers with enough encouragement and guidance to use them effectively. Such programs, while confirming the traditional role of the library as an auxiliary agency to education, might require radical innovations in staff and procedures.

It would be useful to know how these demographic changes have altered reading habits and library policies. There are many gaps and inconsistencies in the available data and much of the important information has simply not been collected. How much are the American people spending for books and libraries; how are they allocating that money between individually purchased books and support for public libraries; and finally, how has the amount of money and its allocation changed over the past decade? Table 1 shows the answers to all of these questions. The total personal consumption figures for books and the total income for public libraries in constant 1954 dollars are included. The table also shows the percentage of increase in the total personal and library expenditures from 1950 to 1960 and the public libraries' share of that total in each of those two years.

While the total Gross National Product increased by 39 per cent

[8] Guy G. Garrison, *Seattle Voters and Their Public Library* (Springfield, Ill.: Illinois State Library, September 1961), Research Series No. 2.

TABLE 1 DISTRIBUTION OF NATIONAL RESOURCES FOR BOOKS AND PUBLIC LIBRARIES
*(In millions of dollars)**

	1950	1960
Consumer expenditures for books†	756	1,280
Total income for public libraries‡	131	280
Total	887	1,560
Percentage of total book expenditures made by public libraries	14.8%	18.0%
Percentage increase in total book expenditures	76%	

* In constant 1954 dollars. U.S. Office of Business Economics, *Survey of Current Business*, July, 1961 (Washington: U.S. Government Printing Office). Table 6, p. 8.
† *Ibid.*, Table 15, p. 14.
‡ *The Bowker Annual of Library and Book Trade Information* (New York: R. R. Bowker Co., 1960 and 1963). The figures for 1960 are averaged from reported 1959 and 1961 data.

between 1950 and 1960,[9] the amount expended on books and public libraries increased by 76 per cent, a much faster rate of growth. Still, it must be recalled that books and libraries occupied a tiny fraction of the GNP, so we are dealing with only the smaller sliver of the economy where gains are perhaps unduly magnified when stated in percentage terms. Nevertheless, this growth is impressive. Even if we assume that the reading audience increased at most by 50 per cent, it is clear that books are being used faster than can be accounted for by a simple increase in population. This is an important fact and difficult to interpret.

The next important thing about the figures in Table 1 is that library funds are such a small part of the total expenditure for books. Note that only 18 per cent of the public's investment in books is made through public libraries. This means that the market is choosing most of the books, not the professional librarian. However, it should be noted that approximately 20 per cent of the total consumer expenditures are for elementary and secondary school texts and work-

[9] U.S. Office of Business Economics, *Survey of Current Business* (Washington: U.S. Government Printing Office, July 1961), Table 5, p. 8.

books.[10] Since this money is spent by the school systems, the total amount spent for books by the individual consumer is smaller than indicated in Table 1.

Perhaps more important is the fact that the share of the public's book dollar that went to public libraries in 1950 is quite close to the share given in 1960. Whether the increase of about 3 per cent is to be interpreted as the library's failure to achieve a greater share of the book dollar, or whether it is to be regarded as a brilliant victory in the face of the paperback book and the book club, or whether it should be seen simply as muddling through, I do not know. The point is that for this period the library has moved forward ever so slightly as a resource for books.

Next we want to know what has happened to the *stock* of books: how many there are, how fast the number has increased, and in what directions. Then we want to know about the *flow* of books: what kinds of books are moving more or less rapidly through the various distribution channels.

It is impossible to make an inventory of the total stock of books in the country.[11] Instead we can assess the annual contribution to that stock as indicated by publishers' sales receipts. Data from the years 1947 and 1958 are readily available, so that we can see the shift in book preferences over approximately the same decade discussed in Table 1. Table 2 shows the percentage of types of books sold during each of the two years and the percentage of change in sales over the ten-year period. Note that these are both paperback and hard-cover books. The categories are those of the book trade.

There is a great deal on which to comment in this table. Most obvious is the order of magnitude of different types of books. In both years sales of textbooks and general adult books lead all other categories. It is quite striking that sales of general adult books should be roughly two to three times the sales of children's books. In the public library circulation figures, the situation is reversed.

10 Data based on share of these texts among all books in Fritz Machlup, *The Production and Distribution of Knowledge* (Princeton: Princeton University Press, 1962), Table 6-3, p. 215.

11 Bolt Beranek and Newman Inc., *Estimates of the Information Content of the World's "Literature,"* Report No. 983, Job No. 11112, submitted to Council of Library Resources, Inc., March 1963.

TABLE 2 NUMBER OF BOOKS SOLD BY PUBLISHERS, 1947–1958
(In thousands)

Item	1947 Number	1947 Per cent	1958 Number	1958 Per cent	Per cent Change 1947–1958
Textbooks and workbooks	139,085	28.6	204,707	22.8	+ 47
Encyclopedias and reference	14,626	3.0	30,620	3.4	+109
Religious	42,543	8.7	70,807	7.9	+ 66
Technical, scientific, and professional	17,467	3.6	23,679	2.6	+ 36
General adult	140,414	28.8	340,853	37.8	+143
General juvenile	53,752	11.0	172,932	19.2	+222
Other	79,329	16.3	56,648	6.3	− 29
Total	487,216	100.0%	900,246	100.0%	
Total change					+ 85%

Source: Fritz Machlup, *The Production and Distribution of Knowledge in the United States* (Princeton: Princeton University Press, 1962), Table VI-3, p. 215.

One should not think that subscription sales of encyclopedias are as small a share as they appear — about 3 per cent of all books. They are expensive, and when Table 2 is recast in terms of publishers' dollar receipts, encyclopedias and reference books comprise 15 per cent of all sales.

The next most impressive thing about Table 2 is the increase in the number of books sold from 1947 to 1958. Eighty-five per cent more books were sold in 1958 than in 1947. (According to Table 1, at approximately the same time there was an increase of 76 per cent in the number of dollars spent on books.) Yet the sales of some types of books hardly increased at all, while others did extremely well. The two kinds of books with a smaller increase in sales were textbooks and scientific, technical, and professional books.

It is no surprise that textbook sales did not increase very much. Considerable effort has been directed to freeing the student from the limitations of the single text and opening the diverse contents of the library to him. It is a tremendous challenge to all libraries to provide the diversity of materials now seen as necessary for modern education. The degree to which the public library should be involved in primary, secondary, and higher education is a question we will consider in the second part of this paper.

The second category of books whose sales have only increased moderately is the scientific-technical and professional group. Given the enormous expansion of science and technology, it seems accurate to say that a 36 per cent increase over the decade represents a decline in the use of books for scientific communication. I am not sure why this is so, but I would suspect that the scientific periodical and the varieties of near-print research reports and memoranda have increasingly become the basic means of communication. Thus if public libraries are to be information centers for the business, technical, and professional communities, they must employ document specialists and information retrievers.

The only other really significant point about Table 2 is that the number of children's books sold has increased faster than any other category, a 222 per cent increase over the decade — perhaps a reflection of changed educational practices and of enormously increased publishing efforts in the juvenile field. Since it is estimated that between 80 and 90 per cent of all juvenile books costing over $1.00 are bought by public libraries, this growth of children's book sales is reflected in the libraries' holdings.

A second important measure of the stock of books is the figure on library holdings. It is difficult to give a meaningful estimate of the number of library books in the country; the only useful estimate is the rate of growth of library holdings. There is fairly good information about libraries in cities of 50,000 or over. These comprise only about 5 per cent of all libraries in the country, but of course these are all the important metropolitan library systems. In 1950 these 225 library systems held 58.6 million volumes and by 1959 the stock had grown to 78.6 million, an increase of 34 per cent.[12] The stock of

[12] U.S. Office of Education, *Statistics of Public Libraries with Populations of 50,000 to 99,999 for 1950*, Circular No. 339 (Washington: U.S. Government Printing Office, April 1952); *Statistics of Public Library Systems in Cities with Popula-*

library books is increasing at a slower rate than the national stock of books. Recall from Table 2 that there was an 85 per cent increase in the number of books sold during the same decade. Perhaps this is as it should be, given the professional standards of book selection in libraries. Without some estimates of quality and some standards for comparison, the only conclusion that can be drawn from the statistics is that the public library is not increasing its stock of books as rapidly as other distribution channels.

It is difficult, however, to come to any conclusion about the quality of the stock of books in the country. In two ways the stock of books seems deficient. The public library, because of its historic commitment to "reach all the people," has by and large been unable to create collections. Main libraries in cities such as New York, Cleveland, and Pittsburgh are the few exceptions. The compromise necessary to provide service to all the various groups of people comprising the clientele of the library has weakened the depth and scope of the collections of most public libraries. This is not inevitable, and shortly I will suggest a way to mitigate the difficulty.

The other deficiency of the public libraries — indeed, of all libraries — is their failure to collect and organize nonbook materials such as original data and finished research reports or memoranda as well as they might. There are mountains of statistical materials — attitude survey data, market research information, routine accounting statistics from industry, government, the courts, hospitals, the schools, and so forth — which are not collected and stored. This is a task beyond the scope of libraries, even metropolitan public libraries, but it must be done somehow. As social scientists increasingly demand such materials, various data bank arrangements will have to be developed.

Now for the problems of the flow of books: what kinds of books are being distributed, and through what channels are which books distributed? The main distribution channels are the book stores, drugstores and newsstand outlets for paperbacks, direct mail from publishers, book clubs, door-to-door salesmen (primarily for encyclo-

---

tions of 50,000 to 99,999: Fiscal Year 1959, PE 15015, August 1960; *Statistics of Public Library Systems in Cities with Populations of 100,000 or More: Fiscal Year 1959,* OE-15014A (Revised), October 1960.

pedias), the schools, libraries of all types, and finally, the secondary flow from individual private collections.

There are no comprehensive statistics showing the relative contributions of these channels to the total flow of books. Some patchwork with available data is necessary; this is not too satisfactory, but it is all we have at the moment. The data in Table 3 are taken from the Hunt survey of 1960. They are abstracted and combined to emphasize channels of distribution rather than types of books. The picture is not complete, because some types of books are omitted and for some channels of distribution we have no information. Next to the raw figures for the number of volumes sold in 1959 is the increase in the volume of sales from 1952 to 1960.

*TABLE 3 DISTRIBUTION OF BOOK SALES**

	Number of Books, 1959 (*In millions of copies*)	Per cent Increase in Sales Volume 1952–1960
Educational†	209	–‡
Adult trade, hard-cover	35	62.4
Adult trade, paperback	10	787.9
Wholesale paperback	252	79.6
Book clubs	74	87.5
Subscription	32	–‡
Juvenile over $1.00	40	158.7
Juvenile under $1.00	153	151.3
Total books	944	91.8

* Reported in the *Bowker Annual,* 1960, pp. 40, 47, 48. Data are from survey of Stanley Hunt for the Book Industry Committee of the Book Manufacturers Institute, 1960.

† All types of texts and workbooks at all levels, from elementary through college.

‡ Data on growth not reported.

Common knowledge makes it possible to deduce the kinds of books which are distributed through various channels. In turn it is possible to judge the number of books sold through these channels. The interesting points about the relative size of the various book channels are the massiveness of the educational component and the smallness of the adult trade sold in book stores. Note that book clubs distribute about twice as many books as do book stores. In terms of growth, the volume of hard-cover books sold in book stores is the smallest of all the channels of distribution listed. The sales of high-quality paperbacks have increased the fastest, and a considerable number of successful paperback book stores have been opened. It is also clear that the so-called "paperback revolution" has lost its rapid growth rate, and so have the book clubs. It should be noted, however, that although the top three book clubs are responsible for about 80 per cent of all book club sales, the number of specialized book clubs has proliferated enormously. Thus, there are various ethnic and religious clubs — Irish, Jewish, French, Catholic and Lutheran book clubs. There are occupationally specialized clubs, such as lawyers', business leaders', mechanical engineers', and real estate brokers' book clubs, and there are special interest clubs, such as art, history, sports, hi-fidelity, horsemanship, science, and science fiction. In 1960 *The Bowker Annual* listed almost 100 adult and about 20 juvenile book clubs. The existence of these specialized clubs underscores the fragmentation of the American reading public into a series of subpublics insulated from each other by the boundaries of their tastes and the absence of a general forum bringing together all book readers.

The flow of books from libraries is easier to define. At least the circulation figures of public libraries are available. However, the growth of other kinds of libraries during the decade was very important. Neither college, university, research, nor public libraries expanded greatly in number, while special libraries — those in industrial corporations, government agencies, and so forth — did grow at a tremendous pace. The number of special libraries increased from about 1,400 in 1959 to close to 2,400 in 1960, an increase of 70 per cent.[13] This growth of special libraries again emphasizes the fragmentation and subdivision of the American reading public into narrow and relatively isolated units.

13 *American Library Directory* (New York: R. R. Bowker Co., 1951), 19th ed., p. ix; *ibid.*, 23rd ed., 1962, p. xiii.

To return to the public library and its part in the flow of books, there are several figures that define the trends. In 1950 public libraries in cities of over 50,000 circulated 174 million books; in 1959 the circulation had increased 50 per cent to 261 million. The new index of circulation prepared at the University of Illinois based on 39 libraries representative of the cities around the country shows the same trend: from 1950 to 1960 their circulation increased by 68 per cent.[14] What must be taken into account, however, is how the populations served by these libraries have grown.

The population served by libraries in cities of over 50,000 increased by only 11 per cent. This is almost exactly the rate of growth of the central cities of the Standard Metropolitan Statistical Areas, as noted at the beginning of this paper. In other words, city libraries, without reaching beyond their natural constituency, have augmented their circulation by five to six times the simple population increase. In the University of Illinois sample of 39 cities, the population served over the decade increased 25 per cent. For these cities, then, circulation grew almost three times as fast as population. This is a significant achievement.

The question arises, however, as to what kinds of books the library is circulating. Two slivers of data provide a partial answer. The first is the old University of Illinois Index of circulation which shows the trends in circulation from 1930 to 1960 for a sample of representative libraries. Over the thirty years there has been a 50 per cent increase in total circulation. During this same period, the circulation of adult fiction declined from 46 per cent to 24 per cent, while the circulation of adult nonfiction remained fairly stable, only increasing from 21 to 26 per cent of the total circulation.[15] These figures imply that the public library is simply responsive to large trends. It has followed the publishing industry's expansion of children's literature and the public demand for children's books. It has reflected the rise of paperback fiction by its diminished circulation of fiction, but it has not developed its nonfiction circulation to any great extent.

14 Data sent to the author personally from the Library Research Center, University of Illinois.

15 University of Illinois Graduate School of Library Science, "Index of American Public Library Circulation," *ALA Bulletin*, Vol. 55 (July–August 1961), p. 646.

The second clue to what kinds of books the library is circulating comes from matching the Dewey decimal classification of all titles published by the American book industry in 1959 with the Dewey classified circulation of the Chicago Public Library for 1962. Such a comparison, though quite rough, allows us to see to what extent the library is circulating different kinds of books from those being offered to the public by the publishers. Table 4 shows a remarkable parallel between the two sets of figures.

The only differences are that religious books are undercirculated compared to new titles and that fine arts books are overcirculated. I do not think anything very substantial about quality can be concluded from this table except that the public library, at least in Chi-

TABLE 4 DEWEY CLASSIFICATION OF NEW NONFICTION TITLES PUBLISHED AND NONFICTION BOOKS CIRCULATED IN CHICAGO

Dewey Classification		Per cent Nonfiction Titles Published, 1959*	Per cent Nonfiction Circulated — Chicago Public Library, 1962†
Generalia	000	3.7	0.7
Philosophy	100	4.3	4.9
Religion	200	10.5	3.3
Social Science	300	12.4	17.0
Languages	400	1.8	1.2
Pure Science	500	9.5	8.7
Applied Science	600	19.0	17.0
Fine Arts	700	6.1	11.0
Literature	800	12.4	13.0
History	900	8.4	11.0
Geography	910	3.6	4.5
Biography	920	7.2	7.7
		99.0	100.0

* R. R. Bowker Co., New York: data published in *Publishers' Weekly*. Reproduced in *Statistical Abstract of the United States*.

† Data submitted by the Chicago Public Library.

cago, is again seen to be offering simply what the publishing industry presents.

There is one last question that will tell us what has been happening to reading: does the reading public really include new sectors of the population or is there much more intensive reading on the part of the normal constituency? This is a vital question. Unfortunately, there is no clear answer as yet, for there has been no comprehensive inventory of reading recently and the partial answers I have collected conflict. The source for data about reading and library use is Berelson's *Library Public*. In brief, Berelson concluded that only about 25 to 30 per cent of the adult population reads a book a month and that about 20 to 30 per cent of adults used a library.[16]

Other surveys support this puzzling conclusion. A 1959 Gallup poll showed that 77 per cent of the sample never read books; that is essentially no change from the studies reviewed in 1948 by Berelson.[17] Several newer studies show no significant increase in the rate of reading. Both Hajda's study in Baltimore and Johnstone's national sample of adults show a level of book reading comparable to that which Berelson found. Hajda found that about 52 per cent of adults have read a book within a year and Johnstone found that 60 per cent of adults had read at least one book within the year. It is true that Johnstone's question — "How many books have you read within the past year?" — invites inflation, but it is still within the order of magnitude of the Hajda study and the new Gallup study which reports that 46 per cent of a national sample have read a book within the year. Table 5 raises the question as to whether the probable increase in reading reaches across all educational level or is restricted to the better educated.

I do not know what to make of these data. Data from sales and circulation indicate that reading has increased dramatically over the decade, but the polls do not show the increase. Who is reading more of what kinds of books and where are they getting them? A new

16 Bernard Berelson, *The Library's Public: A Report of the Public Library Inquiry* (New York: Columbia University Press), 1949, pp. 6, 23.

17 *Ibid.* Berelson's data are from the Field and Peacock's 1949 study of library users as reported in Table 8, showing a total of 22 per cent of the sample registered borrowers; the comparable figure for the 1962 Hopkins registration is 25 per cent (female and male heads of households are combined).

TABLE 5 ADULT READERS BY EDUCATIONAL LEVEL

Study	Less Than High School	Completed High School	Some College or More
Hajda Study			
Per cent reading a book within a year	31 (1,713)	62 (838)	80 (745)
Johnstone Study			
Per cent reporting one or more books read within a year	43 (842)	67 (524)	90 (353)

national inventory of reading is clearly necessary to answer these questions and others that, when put together, would provide an up-to-date and extensive factual background for policy planning. Too often surveys of a community's library system do not indicate what the reading clientele is actually doing about its book needs. There seems to be evidence that reading books is a growing practice in America. It is also clear that the library is keeping abreast of this practice. But is the library doing the job it could do? Tentatively, I think not. It is merely responding to public demands and to the trends of the publishers. I should like to analyze this situation in a little more detail, for the role of the librarian is decisive in the future of book reading. The second part of this paper, therefore, deals with the goals of public libraries.

Goals of the Public Library

The structure of the goals of the public library has not been clearly understood. The reasons for this lie in the history of the public library movement in the United States, which began not so much as a neutral and objective service agency, but as part of a loosely connected series of social movements ranging from the struggle for women's rights to vote and enter the work force to a general reformist and evangelical belief in education and uplift. Fremont Rider, in his short biographical sketch of Melvil Dewey, notes:

> Dewey's great service to the American feminist movement was his stubborn and absolutely unequivocal insistence that women could, should and

would be admitted to his Columbia Library School classes — regardless of rules or orders, trustees or faculty.

All through his life he pleaded for an equal place for women with men in all the world's work, and pleaded for it with passionate and convincing sincerity.[18]

To have some idea of the fervor of the library faith and its general relation to the progressive reformist ideology of the end of the nineteenth century, note the following short section of a report of the 1912 meeting of the American Library Association in Ottawa. It is a summary of the welcoming remarks of the President of the Women's Canadian Club of Ottawa.

She said the preachers, the teachers, the writers and the librarians are four great armies, standing to protect us and to dispel the hydra-headed enemy Ignorance but that she thought of librarians as captains of individual garrisons scattered here and there through towns and cities, who are sending out emissaries among the people and moulding and forming the mental and moral fibre of each community.[19]

Herbert Putnam, Librarian of Congress and formerly Librarian of the Boston Public Library, said at this same meeting, "Our aim is in terms a simple one. It is to bring a book to a reader, to lead a reader to a book."[20]

In the last two decades of the nineteenth century and first two decades of the twentieth, the annual reports of major public libraries contained strong and clear statements that education was the primary goal and that other goals such as providing information and recreational reading were less important. Binding together these goals was a prime article of the library faith, that the library must serve everyone in the community.

This is an important yet ambiguous matter. It is first an affirmation of one of the strongest instinctive responses of the American democratic tradition: that public institutions, especially educational

[18] Fremont Rider, *Melvil Dewey* (American Library Association, 1944), pp. 80, 81.

[19] "Papers and Proceedings of the Thirty-Fourth Annual Meeting of the American Library Association Held at Ottawa, Canada, June 26–July 2, 1912," *ALA Bulletin*, Vol. 6 (July 1912), p. 57.

[20] *Ibid.*, p. 59.

ones, should counteract special privilege and, more crucially, counteract the family transmission of that privilege. The library, therefore, must help those who need an extra boost in the struggle to achieve, if not success, at least opportunity.

The library's goal of reaching everyone has another meaning. It is a peculiar cultural imperialism that was part of the progressive era: everyone should read good books; everyone should develop his capacities to the fullest; and everyone should be educated, freer, and above all, more refined. Excerpts from the redoubtable Dr. Putnam's speech at the 1912 ALA meetings illustrate all of these themes:

> ... democracy means the participation of the community as a whole in the conduct of its affairs.
>
> But democracy ought to mean more: it ought to mean the participation of every individual in its opportunities. And a constitution of society which still left the resources for power and intellectual direction in the hands of the few was in effect an aristocracy. ... Among these resources a chief is education. And the practical monopoly of education, a monopoly which survived after limitations of caste were removed and the opportunities for wealth became widely diffused meant a monopoly of influence also. Against it the free public school, the easily available college, the procurable newspaper and magazine and the free public library fought and are fighting their fight in the interest of ... the individual ... to equip him as an independent and co-equal unit.[21]

In the early days of library development the desire to serve the whole community was both meaningful and useful, if for no other reason than that it spurred the motivation to build the public library. But much has changed since those early days. Nearly all of the reform movements died of success, and thus much of the steam behind the library efforts was lost. In addition, the general level of affluence in American life, the relative leveling of income differentials, and the widespread accessibility of books from other channels have robbed the public library movement of some of its most important direction and internal drive.[22]

Public libraries have become large, multipurpose organizations,

21 *Ibid.*, pp. 60 ff.

22 Burton Clark, "Organizational Adaptation and Precarious Values: A Case Study," *American Sociological Review*, Vol. 21 (June 1956), pp. 327–336.

highly differentiated and serving specialized audiences. Have they done what multipurpose organizations always must do, that is, assign a priority ranking to their goals? Generally speaking, they have not. One of the main reasons they have not done so is the continued belief in the now almost irrelevant ideological statement that the library must serve everybody. Moreover, after studying the statements of library objectives and examining some important library surveys, I conclude that they do not understand the basic economic fact that they have limited resources and consequently must assign priorities to the various kinds of services they wish to offer.[23] It is simply impossible for the library to do everything at once. It cannot serve all the people in the community and do any of them justice.

A careful scrutiny of library literature over the past fifteen years failed to reveal any systematic awareness that the expanding array of library goals could be or should be ranked into some conscious priority system, with money and staff resources allocated accordingly. Here is a typical recommendation from a survey of a state library system:

> The first element of good public library service is its universal availability, because such availability helps to insure the ideal of opportunity for every individual. . . . A public library is effective only to the extent that it focuses its program on and is closely integrated with the community it serves. Circulating books to one portion of the community, i.e., children or housewives, is not serving the entire community.[24]

A recent report of the Los Angeles County Library is also typical. Their goal is that adopted by the Council of the ALA: "Public Library Service that will help every American discharge his obligations as an informed citizen and achieve full self-development."[25]

[23] The only clear call to set priorities that I have found is that stated by Berelson at the conclusion of his *Library's Public.* It is saddening to observe, however, that Robert Leigh's summary volume of the Public Library Inquiry did not echo this theme, but rather reverted to the rhetoric of the past — the library must serve everyone.

[24] Gretchen K. Schenk, *Public Library Service in Nevada, a Survey with Recommendations* (n.p., 1958).

[25] American Library Association, Co-ordinating Committee on Revision of Public Library Standards, *Public Library Service: A Guide to Evaluation, with Minimum Standards* (Chicago: American Library Association), 1956.

The Los Angeles report continues by saying:

> . . . our continuing purpose is to furnish readers with an expanding and broad-based book collection administered by a highly competent staff and, over a period of time, provide functional and well designed modern buildings throughout the system.[26]

Los Angeles was also thinking of a large-scale branch building program, and the report also stressed increasing service to students, as well as efforts to shape the collection into "vast reservoirs of cultural and recreational materials."

The annual reports of a sample of medium and large-city public libraries reveal one or both of these failures: either a failure to allocate energies according to a priority ranking of goals, or a retreat from high-level goal statements into administrative objectives of efficiency or expansion. The only time there appears to be a statement of high-level goals is when the libraries are seeking money, and then they make promises that sound like the library movement of the old days. Because there has been so little concentrated effort in determining goals, the library has become socially invisible. Trying to do everything means not only a dissipation of energies but also a loss of a well-served and loyal clientele who will promote and defend the library. Therefore, both to win support in the community and really to do an effective job, it seems imperative that public libraries re-examine their multipurpose situation and set clear priorities for their objectives.

It is neither possible nor desirable to spell out a national program or national standards. Each public library must determine its priorities on the joint basis of its own community's needs and power structure. If the business community is the leading elite in a community, and if its information needs are not met adequately by special libraries, then the librarian might propose, for example, that for the next five years the library concentrate its efforts on becoming the central information center for the professional and business community by providing a specialized book collection, reference, and research services. Or if, in another city, the population shifts

[26] *Los Angeles County Public Library Biennial Report,* 1959–1961, No. 48/49, p. 3.

have left a large population that is deprived of educational and cultural resources, for example Negro and Spanish-speaking groups, it might very well be the central mission of that library system to become the educational and cultural auxiliary to whatever agencies are working to improve the opportunities for the deprived groups. Or if, in still another city, a sector of community leaders is concerned with improving cultural facilities, the librarian might propose to ally the library with the institutions of culture, the art museum, and the musical organizations, and to devote its energies to collecting high-quality literature and expanding its nonbook programs to include poetry readings and film exhibits. It may also want to coordinate its book exhibits and buying with the other organized cultural activities in the city.

There are many more alternatives. The key point is to put a conscious priority on certain library objectives and press forward in concentrated bursts for a period of some years, picking up support and doing an effective job, then moving on to the next target. The alternative is to drift with the tide of fluctuating and residual public interests.

ALLISON DAVIS

SOCIAL-CLASS PERSPECTIVES

Working-class people, especially those in the lowest, most deprived class, read fewer books than middle-class people, as well as a different type of book. They differ from middle-class people in their language and in the principal use which they make of language, as well as in their cultural attitudes toward books. They and their children use libraries much less than do middle-class people.[1] A major problem of urban libraries, then, is their relative ineffectiveness in attracting adults and children from the lower half of the working class.

During the past decade, the American city has become increasingly the province of the working class. In New York, Washington, D. C., Philadelphia, Chicago, Cleveland, Detroit, Los Angeles, and most southern cities, about 70 per cent of the pupils in the public schools come from working-class families. Nearly half of this 70 per cent are children from so-called "slum" families, the lower group within the working class, consisting chiefly of unskilled or semiskilled workers.[2]

To begin to solve the problem of attracting low-income people to libraries, one must understand the culture and the basic way of life of the lower class, and how this culture differs from that of middle-class people. One needs to understand the cultural perspective of

1 W. Lloyd Warner and Paul S. Lunt, *The Social Life of a Modern Community* (Vol. I of Yankee City Series; New Haven: Yale University Press, 1941), pp. 378–406.

2 Allison Davis, "The Future Education of Children from Low Socio-Economic Groups," in *New Dimensions for Educational Progress*, ed. Stanley Elam (Bloomington, Indiana: Phi Delta Kappa, 1963), pp. 27–54.

lower-class people and the relative importance of cognitive and emotional needs in their lives.

Many lower-class people use and understand language which is highly abstract, and no doubt many of the great writers who were reared in lower-class families had a parent who spoke this more conceptual abstract English. But the fact emphasized here is that there is a difference between the proportion of lower-class and middle-class people who speak this more abstract language, and the difference is in favor of middle-class people.

Cultural descriptions have to be made in terms of norms or averages, that is, of some over-all measure. Using the arithmetic mean to describe group behavior, we find that on verbal problems, both in tests and in oral language, lower-class children, on the average, exhibit less skill in the solution of abstract verbal problems and in understanding or using abstract oral English.

In research conducted in 1946 by Professor David Ray Stone on the manifestations of intelligence by middle-class and lower-class children of ages nine to ten and thirteen to fourteen, he discovered that from 60 per cent to 80 per cent of lower-class children and middle-class children agreed in their definition of words on a multiple-choice test. The major difference between the two classes existed between their success on words which could be pictured (such as "nose," "ice," "locomotive," and "orchestra") and words which could not be pictured (such as "thought," "odor," "liberty," "concede," "dexterity," and "doubt"). Both groups defined the picturable, or concrete, words more successfully than the abstract words. The middle-class children, however, were far more successful than those of the lower class in defining the abstract words. The difference was statistically significant at the 1 per cent level. The middle-class children chose the correct definition of the abstract words in 24 per cent more cases than did the lower-class children.[3]

Kaniz Ataullah, working with me in a study of children's solutions of verbal problems, found that lower-class children solved verbal problems requiring generalization less successfully than did middle-

[3] David Ray Stone, *Certain Verbal Factors in the Intelligence-Test Performance of High and Low Social Status Groups* (unpublished doctoral dissertation, Department of Education, University of Chicago, 1946).

class children. The class difference was significant at the .01 to .025 level of probability, depending upon the problem. There was no significant difference between lower-class and middle-class children, however, on highly abstract cognitive problems, such as analogies and probabilities (of the Piaget type), when these problems were expressed in words symbolizing *objects* and *people* and their relationship.[4]

Life does not consist only of rational and other cognitive efforts to describe and embrace reality, however. Nor is abstract language always the most effective language. The language of *Othello,* usually regarded as Shakespeare's most advanced stage in dramatic language, is neither markedly abstract nor cognitive. Unlike *Hamlet* or *King Lear, Othello* is written in dramatic language, derived from and leading to action, with none of the irrelevant and reflective soliloquies of *Hamlet,* or the windy bombast of *King Lear.*[5]

Many middle-class people, especially those in academic life, believe that facility in standard English is the highest expression of mental ability. In our training as teachers, professors, and librarians, we have been misled by the social-class evaluations of types of language usage and of types of writing. But facility in a particular language results more from cultural association, from life in a given national and class group, and more particularly from life in a family which exhibits and emphasizes such linguistic skill, than from exceptional mental ability. Language is an ancient and highly formalized system of cultural and, therefore, of learned behavior.

Lower-class dialects are regarded as "uncultured" by middle-class and upper-class people, that is, as lacking refinement, sophistication, and skill. Social anthropologists and comparative linguists do not agree with this view, however. Edward Sapir, generally recognized as having been the most perceptive and creative comparative linguist of our time, considered it very doubtful that facility in modern English required any greater mental ability than did

4 Kaniz Ataullah, *Cultural Influences upon Children's Solutions of Verbal Problems* (unpublished doctoral dissertation, Department of Education, University of Chicago, 1950).

5 Furness Variorum Edition of the individual tragedies of Shakespeare. *See also* the critical works of George Saintsbury on Shakespeare.

many so-called primitive languages of preliterate peoples, or than lower-class dialects.

The following words of Sapir should be pondered by every teacher and librarian [italics mine]:

> The lowliest South African Bushman speaks in the forms of a rich symbolic system that is in essence perfectly comparable to the speech of the cultivated Frenchman. . . . The sort of linguistic development that parallels the historic growth of culture and which, in its later stages, we associate with literature is, at best, but a superficial thing. The fundamental groundwork of language — the development of a clear-cut phonetic system, the specific associations of speech elements with concepts, *and the delicate provision for the formal expression of all manner of relations* — all this meets us rigidly perfected and systematized in every language known to us. *Many primitive languages have a formal richness, a latent luxuriance of expression, that eclipses anything known to the languages of modern civilization.* . . .
>
> Both simple and complex types of language, of an indefinitive number of varieties, may be found spoken at any desired level of cultural advance. When it comes to linguistic form, Plato walks with the Macedonian swineherd, Confucius with the head-hunting savage of Assam.[6]

Swadesh has pointed out that every people has developed a language capable of expressing every type of intellectual and emotional concept:

> We have to conclude that inflexion, in particular, and linguistic structure in general have nothing to do with the advancement of a people. All languages in the world, today and within the historical period, have, and had, structures sufficiently flexible to express every category of thought which the human being can conceive.[7]

There are, of course, two forms of language. The first is the spoken language, which is the original, more basic, and creative aspect of language. The second is the written language. Written language is, as Sapir called it, "a symbol of a symbol"; that is, written language is an incomplete and clumsy attempt to symbolize the spoken language, which itself is a far richer and more complete group of

6 Edward Sapir, *Language* (New York: Harcourt, Brace & World, Inc., 1939), pp. 22, 234.

7 Morris Swadesh, *La Nueva Filologia,* Vol. 4, Coleccion "Single XX" (Biblioteca del Maestro Mexico, El Nacional, 1941), p. 41.

symbols of the outer and inner realities of man's life. Middle-class people, notably professional writers, teachers, and librarians, have invested a kind of traditional worship in the written language, but all students of language agree that both the enrichment of language and the change (or growth and drift) of language arise chiefly from the spoken usage of the people. As inheritors of the English language, we are in somewhat the position of the *nouveaux riches* who look with shame and scorn upon those who gave them energy and vitality, the masses of the people.

In literature itself there is a tendency in America to regard Holmes, Lowell, Henry James, and Marquand — all born in the upper class — not as greater poets and novelists than American authors born in lower estate, but as writers of a more subtle, sophisticated, and acceptable English, and as being able better to stand comparison with the best born in England, who are thought to write the best English. But Shakespeare was born in the lower-middle class and Samuel Johnson, Wordsworth, Coleridge, Keats, Thackeray, George Eliot, Whitman, Mark Twain, and O'Neill had no pretensions to aristocracy.

Abraham Lincoln was the lower-class son of two illiterate parents. In spite of his boyhood in an illiterate family and his adolescence in a lower-class rural group, during his thirties and forties Lincoln learned to write prose which in his best debates with Douglas attains the highest level of reasoned and lucid exposition, in the tradition of Burke. In his later speeches he attained an equally high level of spiritual and emotional power, in a style with the inevitability of the King James translation of the Bible, but distinctly his own.

The criterion of good English, as Samuel Daniel said in 1602 in his *Defence of Rime,* an eloquent championing of the native English usage and meters against imitations of Latin meters, is common usage, the language of the people. It is the people, not the grammarians or the academicians, who have developed the English language. The people have always, in every culture, created both language and the myths and songs which professional writers have organized and polished. Homer is a name for the art of generations of illiterate folk poets and singers whose creations were integrated and rephrased for the literate by the authors of the *Iliad.* Modern composers have used folk songs and dances as themes for learned compositions which often lack the vitality and emotional depth of the folk original. Dvorak's *New World Symphony,* for instance, is a well-meant effort to present the theme of a Negro folk spiritual in symphonic style, but lacks the power of the folk original.

Admittedly, it is the music of the spirituals rather than their words which has gained universal recognition as art. More than thirty years ago, Professor Guy Johnson pointed out that many of the phrases in the spirituals are reminiscent of Protestant hymns and of Anglo-American folk songs. Like other artists, the Negro folk singers borrowed and improved what they found at hand. Even the words, however, have at times a genuinely poetic imagery or feeling seldom found even in the lyrics of the songs of the literate.

> My Lord, what a morning,
> When the stars begun to fall!

or

> Were you there when they pierced Him in the side?
> Oh, sometimes it causes me to tremble, tremble.

or

> Sometimes I feel like a motherless child
> A long ways from home.

or

> Oh, freedom, Oh, freedom!
> Before I'd be a slave, I'd be buried in my grave
> And go home to my Lord
> And be free!

But inevitably the richest artistic expression of the illiterate creator was in music. Many of the superverbal emotional and spiritual meanings of man's life are expressed in the tones, shadings, and contrasts of this music. The symbol-system which the lower-class Negro has mastered, and in the use of which he exhibits both subtlety and profundity, is that of the sung and played song.

The choice of a symbol-system in which to express thought, feeling, and fantasy, therefore, depends not only upon the individual, but also upon the cultural values and perspectives in which he has been trained by his group. The basic problem is not so much a matter of the degree to which the expression is abstract or specific, as of a perspective upon life which emphasizes ratiocination, on the one hand, or action and emotion, on the other. Every dialect, every type of symbol system, abstracts and generalizes. In painting, a line is a high level of abstraction which children learn to use successfully only after the initial stage of emphasis upon color and smudges. In language, the word "house" is an abstraction based upon a very large number of observations and comparisons of many types of structures. There are no concrete words. All spoken words are symbols. Many words which the lower-class child uses are highly abstract symbols of relationships such as "bedside," "with," "ours," or "half." The problem of the schools and libraries, therefore, is how to develop the power of lower-class children to abstract and generalize in a way to increase their interest and skill in speaking standard English and in reading. In order to understand this difficult problem of acculturation, one needs to understand first the differences between lower-class and middle-class cultures.

The study of American social classes has become a very complex field. This approach to the comparative, or differential, psychology of our social strata has been used in the study of American moral controls, familiar organization and mores, child rearing, adolescent personality, projective responses, sex behavior, illness, politics, rackets, industrial conflict, the public educational system, the courts, the churches, the organizations, the processes involved in rising in the world or falling in the world, and in still other major areas of behavior. In the study of socialization, the social-class approach has been developed systematically in the attempt to understand the processes by which human beings learn their social drives and perspectives, their value systems, their emotional patterns, and their form of logical inference.[8]

Social classes essentially maintain barriers against intimate social participation. Those individuals, families, and social cliques which refer to each other in popular language as "nice" or "respectable" seldom have any intimate association, either at work or in their

[8] Allison Davis, *Social-Class Influences upon Learning* (The Inglis Lecture, 1948; Cambridge, Massachusetts: Harvard University Press, 1948). Also: K. Eells, A. Davis, R. J. Havighurst, V. Herrick, and R. Tyler, *Intelligence and Cultural Differences* (Chicago: University of Chicago Press, 1951).

homes, with any people from those families which are vulgarly called "common," "ignorant," or "low." People from the "wrong side of the tracks" have no intimate association in any form, as equals, with people from the "right side of the tracks." People from the slums are barred from social participation with both the gold coast and the "respectable," middle-class suburbia. Indeed, slum people also are stigmatized and avoided by the lower–middle-class respectable people who may live in the same block. Finally, the bottom group is likewise avoided by "the poor, but honest and clean" families, as they think of themselves, that is, the top group in the working class.

People cannot learn their mores, social drives, and values — their basic culture — from books. One can learn a particular culture and a particular moral system only from those people who know and exhibit this behavior in frequent relationships with the learner. If a child can associate intimately with no one but slum adults and children, he can learn only slum culture. The pivotal meaning of social classes to the student of behavior, therefore, is that they limit and systematize the learning environment of their members. Thus each class has developed its own characteristic and adaptive form of the American basic culture. Each member of a social class learns this cultural behavior from his family, his gang or play group, his social clique, and his other intimate groups.

Because the slum individual usually is responding to a different physical economic, and cultural reality from that in which the middle-class individual is trained, the slum individual's habits and values also must be different, if they are to be realistic. The behavior which we regard as "delinquent" or "shiftless" or "unmotivated" in slum groups is usually a perfectly realistic, adaptive, and in slum life respectable, response to reality.[9]

By restricting an individual's intimate social relationships, therefore, our social class system narrows his learning and training environment. His social interests and goals, as well as his symbolic world and its evaluation, are largely selected from the narrow culture of that class with which he can associate freely.

Middle-class people maintain, organize, and administer American

9 Allison Davis, *op. cit.*, 1948.

life. The lower–middle-class are the backbone of our society; the upper-middles are the brain and the eyes of the society. Almost all of the good things in American life, as we in education evaluate it, are the achievements of middle-status persons. Care of and pride in property, careful child-training with emphasis upon renunciation and sacrifice for future gains, long and arduous education, development of complex and demanding skills, working and learning one's way up in the complicated processes of business, industry, government, and education — all of them are administered (but not controlled) by the upper-middle class in the American status system.

The culture of the middle-status group is highly institutionalized; the church, the organizations, the school, and formal associations of all types are the basic integrating structures in their society. Along with this highly organized structure goes a marked emphasis upon attainment. As compared with both the lower- and higher-status levels, then, the middle group is more highly organized and its members are more deeply motivated — by all institutions in the middle class — to achieve.[10]

This cultural emphasis upon achievement arises largely from social insecurity: in lower-middle groups it arises largely from the fear of loss of occupation or respectability, which would plunge the family into lower-class life; in upper-middle groups, from the fact that, unlike upper-class people, upper-middles are not born to highest status, but must achieve it in the face of social stigmas and punishment, if it is to be theirs.

The middle-class way, with its emphasis upon respectability and morality, upon property, money, and other symbols of attainment, upon organizational ties which dramatize one's adherence to group goals, upon self-improvement through education, or book clubs, or art and music clubs, and upon community improvement through the church, the civic organizations, and the school, is carried on by people who are culturally motivated to work and to renounce or postpone gratifications in order to achieve. To propel the child along this apparently endless route of socialization — so that he may attain

10 Allison Davis, *Psychology of the Child in the Middle Class* (Horace Mann Lecture, University of Pittsburgh, 1960; Pittsburgh: University of Pittsburgh Press, 1961).

a physician's skills, let us say — the middle-status family uses pressures and goals which build anxiety. The child is taught by a well-defined and relatively severe training to strive for the expected or allowed age, sex, or class status, or to attempt to gain a higher age, or school, or social-class status. As the child goes through adolescence, furthermore, he is gradually inducted by parents, teachers, and age-mates into the adult pattern of class behavior. Near the end of high school or at the beginning of his college career, he is urged to begin serious study and preparation for an occupation which will maintain the family's status or improve it. A girl is oriented toward either a decent, good, or brilliant marriage or a skilled or professional occupation.

In working-class families, however, the child learns to seek other pleasures and to want other types of prestige. Growing up in the street culture of blighted areas, living in tenements and kitchenettes, the child of our white and colored slums learns a characteristic pattern of ambitions, pleasures, and habits. From his earliest days, in contrast to the middle-class infant, he usually gains more organic pleasure from life.

Not only is his organic life expressed more directly, but also his basic psychological responses are less frustrated. He is allowed to fight when he is angry, and to laugh when he is triumphant. Frequently he fights even his brothers and sisters. He does not have to accept the false peace between brothers which middle-class parents severely impose. Physical aggression is regarded as normal. Because fighting is common both in his family and in his neighborhood, he learns to take a blow and to give one.

His parents believe that beatings are the normal way of controlling a child or a wife. Thus he gets his thrashings regularly and learns not to fear them. Because his punishment is chiefly physical, he is spared the constant attacks of prolonged guilt, and the fears of losing parental love, which middle-class parents continually arouse, and maintain over long periods, in training their children.

The poor working-class child also has his share of fear and worry. His family is more often struck by disease and by separation. Their chronic poverty breeds fear of eviction, of homelessness, and — most constant of all his fears — of starvation. On the other hand, his family and his gang teach him not to be afraid of a fight, not to be intimidated by the teacher and the police, and not to fear injury or death as keenly as a middle-class child. The child in working-class families is less stimulated by his culture to be fearful and guilty.

He also grows up faster, in the sense of achieving personal maturity. He is not protected from the crises of life. He sits with the ill and the dying. Even as a six-year-old, he listens to family discussions of unemployment, desertion, and adultery. He lives fast, in a society where he will become a man or woman at thirteen or fourteen.

The culture of our slums also differs from that of middle-class groups in its concepts of manliness and womanliness. The slum boy will learn to be more male: coarser, more aggressive physically, more openly sexual, than the middle-class boy. The slum girl will learn to be more female: more outspoken, bolder sexually, more expressive of her impulses and her emotions than the girl trained in middle-class culture. Thus, by the time the underprivileged child is fourteen or fifteen, he has learned a deep cultural motivation which differs at many points from that of middle-class adolescents.

When the masses of children from disadvantaged cultures are confronted by the school's demand for speed in learning materials which are intrinsically lacking in power to motivate them, they become retarded. We know that one-third of the white children of unskilled and semiskilled families in a Midwestern city already are retarded in grade placement by the time they are nine or ten years old. By the time white children from these lowest occupational groups are ten years old, they are about two years behind the children from the top occupational families in reading. Negro eighth-grade children of the lowest economic group are about a year behind the lowest white economic group in reading. In fact, by the time they are three years old most children from the lower socioeconomic groups already are inferior in verbal skills to those from the middle class. It is inevitable, therefore, that starting at the primary-school level, low-status children should perform less well on tests and on the verbal aspects of the curriculum.

Moreover, after the primary grades, the superiority of the middle-class child over the low-status child in verbal skills and academic habits increases even faster. The reasons are clear: the pace set by his parents and teacher and his opportunities to learn language increase more rapidly than the similar pressures and opportunities of the low-status child. By the time these two cultural groups have reached secondary school, the low-status students are farther behind the middle economic group of students than they have ever been. This retardation exists in all areas of language and the curriculum.

All authorities on this subject, beginning with Alfred Binet, who used working-class children in Geneva as the sample upon which the first modern intelligence tests were standardized, have agreed that the academic performance of children from the lower economic groups is characterized by:

1. Their relative lack of attention to the problem as a whole, and to its details. In research on an individual test of problem-solving ability I conducted with Robert D. Hess, we were struck by the fact that in the test situation the average six-year-old child from the low economic groups looked out of the window or at the pictures on the wall, or sat passively, while the average middle-class child asked questions about what was expected of him, handled the toys and other test materials, and repeatedly asked whether he had made the correct response. The lack of attention by low economic groups is a cultural factor, and is related to their lack of identification with the school, its activities, and its teachers.
2. Their lack of apparent interest in and desire to learn the school activities and tasks.
3. Their lack of competitive drive and confidence with respect to achieving in the classroom.
4. Their relatively poor work habits.

The lack of attention and of desire to learn and to compete in school on the part of the low-income groups results to some extent from their cultural handicap. They discover at the very beginning of their school life that they do not know many objects, words, pictures, and concepts which most of the middle-class children know.

An equally powerful deterrent to achievement, however, is their fear and distrust of the teacher and their failure to identify with this stranger and his or her behavior. The lack of attention, lack of desire to learn, and lack of competitive drive in school are expressions of urgent realities: of fear, of feelings of inadequacy, and of the consequent resentment toward the teacher and the school tasks.

The principal emphasis in the preschool and primary grades, therefore, should be placed upon the establishment of a strong relationship of trust and mutual acceptance. The first step in education is to train the pupil to like the teacher. If he does, he will later learn to respect the teacher and will want to win his or her approval. It is generally true that middle-class children have this positive feeling for their teachers, in spite of frequent parental criticism of them.

Informal activities such as reading stories and playing games, allowing the child freedom to tell his own stories about his own life or fantasies, in whatever words he knows, songs, dances, and little plays can establish a bridge between the culture of the teacher and that of the low-status child. Across this bridge the teacher can lead the child into new learning and new behavior, into a new world of letters, numbers, and writing which now become invested with the importance and the cathexis which the child attaches to the teacher and whatever he or she values. From the good relationship with the teacher comes interest in the school, in the primers, and even in the workbooks. It is this spark, struck by the relationships with the teacher, which illuminates and enlivens the world of the mind, whether in the first grade or in graduate school. Therefore we need to bring the child from a low economic group into a relationship with a middle-class teacher as early as possible, and to structure this relationship to make it rewarding to both pupil and teacher.

HOWARD S. BECKER

*NONCOLLEGE YOUTH**

When we talk of education, we ordinarily refer to the conventional institutions in which it is carried on: elementary schools, secondary schools, colleges and universities, graduate and professional schools. But this a narrow and class-biased view. It allows us to talk only about some of the things people learn and some of the places they learn them. For many people, conventional schools are not the only places in which learning occurs. We need, therefore, to ask more general questions, of which questions about conventional educational institutions are special cases. What do people learn as they grow up in our society? Where do they learn it? What do they want to learn? What must they learn if they are to achieve certain things in life? What opportunities have they for learning the things they need to know?

Rather than trying to answer all these questions for all kinds of learning, I will restrict myself to the kind of learning necessary for, to put it colloquially, "making out" in adult life. I will be concerned with the years after high school, the years in which adolescent boys and girls become adult men and women. I will be concerned with what it means, in a public way, to grow up in our society: how one learns the things and acquires the skills needed both to become and to feel oneself to be a mature adult. Social class differences influence this process and, because we know more about the middle class than the lower class in this regard, I will adopt the strategy of summariz-

* The first section of this paper was originally published as "What Do They Really Learn in College?" *Trans-action,* I (May 1964), pp. 14–17. *Trans-action* is a publication of the Community Leadership Project, Washington University, St. Louis, Missouri.

ing some of what we know about the middle class and then speculating about what may be true of the lower class.

Our society distingushes many categories of people according to age. Following anthropological usage, we can call these categories age-grades. For each age-grade, people have some sense of what is characteristic and appropriate for a member of it to do and be. These conceptions are held both by others and by members of the age-grade itself. To move into the next higher age-grade successfully one must convince others and oneself that he is entitled to make the move. The conviction is established by showing that one has the appropriate skills and knowledge.

I will be concerned to show that most of what the middle-class youth needs to know can be learned in college, while some of the things the lower-class youth needs to know are not ordinarily taught him by the institutions with which he comes in contact. Indeed, after surveying the educational institutions, conventional and otherwise, with which lower-class postadolescents come into contact, I will conclude that there are a number of things that need to be done which no institutions are now doing.

Those Who Go to College: The Middle Class

Most middle-class boys and girls graduate from high school and go on to college. Many, perhaps most, college-goers learn in college precisely what they need to know to get along as adults in a middle-class world. The middle-class worlds of business and the professions demand a number of specific skills and abilities, and the experience of college is such as to provide college students with training in precisely those skills and abilities. I shall discuss a number of the demands made by the adult middle-class world, indicating in each case how the world of the college is organized to provide relevant training. Most of what I will talk about is not conventionally regarded as an important part of the college curriculum; nevertheless, these are matters which are important for college students while they are in school and afterwards. They know it and act accordingly.[1]

1 In speaking about college students, I shall rely on the study of undergraduates at the University of Kansas made by myself in collaboration with Blanche

Independence from Home. Ours is one of the most mobile societies ever known. People move frequently and they move great distances. Unlike nomadic groups, they do not move together, taking their families and communities with them. They move because opportunity beckons elsewhere and it beckons to individuals, not groups. (It is sometimes the case, however, that people, moving individually, will gravitate to the same areas of their new community, so that some semblance of the old can be restored in a new place. I am told that Los Angeles contains many such colonies of people of a particular ethnic background and from the same home town who have somehow re-formed in a cluster in some area of the city.)[2]

Moving for the sake of opportunity is very common in the middle class. As more and more people enter itinerant professions or go to work for one of the national organizations which ships its men around from city to city, more and more members of the middle class find themselves as young adults leaving their homes, neighborhoods, and families behind and setting out for new territory. Friends, instead of being furnished almost automatically by family connections and neighborhood contiguity, must be made without that help. To make the break from family and community requires an independence of spirit that does not come naturally.

Going away to college provides a rehearsal for the real thing, an opportunity to be away from home and friends, to make a new life among strangers, while still retaining the possibilities of affiliation with the old. In the dormitory, and even more in the fraternity and sorority, one finds himself on his own but at the same time surrounded by strangers who may become friends. One has the experience of learning to shift for oneself, of making friends among strangers.

Further, all the little chores that one's family performed now have to be taken care of in some other way. One gets one's own meals, takes care of one's own room, makes one's own bed, cleans one's own

---

Geer and Everett C. Hughes. The study was financed by the Carnegie Corporation of New York and carried out under the auspices of Community Studies, Inc., of Kansas City, Missouri. Dean George Waggoner of the University was particularly helpful to us while we were carrying out the study. I want to thank Blanche Geer for her helpful comments on an earlier draft of this paper.

2 I am indebted for this point to Santo F. Camilleri.

clothes. These are small things but, until one has learned to do them, things which may be difficult. They are a kind of training for the passage from home, whether it is geographical or simply the making of a new home upon marriage. Going to college provides the opportunity for this kind of playing at moving away from home for good and prepares the youngster for the world he will have to live in.

Dating, Marriage, and Poise. We normally expect young people to achieve some kind of workable relationship with members of the opposite sex, to learn how to get along with them, and eventually to choose or be chosen for marriage. For the middle-class youth, the problem is complicated by the requirement of the adult work world into which he will move that he choose a wife who will be "culturally adequate" for the circles in which his business or profession will require him to move. He must acquire the ability to attract and marry the kind of woman who can run a proper house for him and entertain for him. This means, of course, that women must learn how to perform these functions in an adequate middle-class way. It means that both men and women must learn the kind of manners, poise, and cultural skills necessary to move in such a world and to attract such a mate.

Again, the college (and particularly the large state university) provides the proper kind of training. Although it is not a standard part of the curriculum, training in manners, poise, and cultural skills is given in a wide variety of places on the campus. Fraternities and sororities specialize in it. Pledges are taught in formal classes how to introduce themselves to strangers, how to ask for a date or accept one, how to behave on a date, how to handle silverware at a formal dinner, and so on. (The necessity for this training is obvious if one watches incoming freshmen during Orientation Week. The people who prepare dinners for these students know that, in order to avoid embarrassment, they had better not serve any strange dishes which require more than rudimentary skill with silver.) Formal training is reinforced by constant practice. A stranger who walks into a fraternity house finds himself assaulted by a stream of young men rushing up to introduce themselves, fearing that if they do not one of the active members will punish them.

The dating system and the round of formal and informal social functions provided by both the Greek system and the university proper afford a fine training ground for meeting the opposite sex and finding a proper mate. Some students are required to have a certain minimum number of dates per month; most students feel some vague pressure to date, even when they find it anxiety-provoking. By participating in a round of parties and social functions, students learn the kind of manners and poise necessary for the social life of the country club or civic organization, skills that will stand them in good stead in their later middle-class lives.

Many, though by no means all, students receive training in dealing socially with "important people." Fraternities, dormitories, and other kinds of student groups make a practice of inviting important people, both campus personages and visitors, to meet with them. Students may have experience interacting with the governor of the state, the chancellor of the university, national political figures, or important visitors from overseas.

Two qualifications are necessary. First, many students learn manners, poise, and similar skills long before they reach college. Some have gone to good preparatory schools and many receive similar training in their own homes. Second, not everyone who goes to college acquires social skills. Some colleges are not set up with the array of organizations characteristic of the University of Kansas. And not all Kansas students receive this training. The ones who are most likely to receive it are those who belong to fraternities and sororities and those who are active in the world of extracurricular activities. Students not in these categories often receive a good deal of social training too, but it is among them that one finds students who slip through without it.

Work Skills. The middle-class occupational world demands a number of generalized work skills from its recruits. They must, first of all, acquire skills needed for their prospective occupations which the university is set up to teach. It may be that they need to learn the analytic techniques of chemistry or engineering; they may need to learn the skills of reading, writing, and the use of a library. Whatever it is, the university has courses which teach them some of the knowledge and techniques necessary to hold a job. (We must not overdo this. Many businesses, industries, and professional and graduate schools feel that the undergraduate college cannot, or at least does not, teach the required skills in the proper way. They prefer to train their recruits from scratch. To this end, many firms have in-service training programs which provide the specific knowledge recruits need.)

More important than the specific knowledge and techniques necessary for entrance into an occupation is a more generalized kind of work skill, one that in older days was referred to as "stick-to-itiveness." The recruit to the middle-class occupational world must have the ability to see a job through from beginning to end, to start a project and keep his attention and energy focused on it until it is completed. The ability to get things done does not come naturally to young people; it is a hard-won skill. In acquiring it, the middle-class youth must learn to defer immediate gratifications for those that are longer in coming, to give up the pleasures of the moment for the larger rewards that await a big job well done. Most students have not had to learn this in high school, where the parade of daily requirements and assignments places the emphasis on receiving the immediate gratification of having done a particular day's job well. For many students, it is only when one reaches college that one is required to plan ahead in units of four or five months, keeping attention focused on the long-range goal of passing the course without the constant prodding of the daily assignment. (This is not to deny that many colleges, particularly in the freshman and sophomore years, mimic the pattern of daily assignments typical of the high school.) In learning to organize himself well enough to get a good grade in a college course, in learning to keep his mind on one job that long, the college student learns the middle-class skill of getting things done, so important in business and industry.

Finally, the middle-class world demands of those who enter it that they be able to juggle several things at once, that they be able to handle several jobs at one time, keeping them straight as they successfully finish all of them. One must learn to manage his time successfully and not fritter it away in actions that produce no reward. At least some college students get magnificent training in how to budget time and energy. The kind of student, of whom there are many, who does well in his courses and at the same time is, let us say, a high-ranking officer in several campus-wide organizations and an officer of his fraternity or dormitory, learns that he cannot waste his time if he is to achieve anything. He learns to set aside particular times for studying and to allow nothing to intervene; he learns to handle organizational matters with dispatch; he learns to give up or strictly ration the joys of watching television and drinking beer with the boys. He learns, in short, how to have a time for everything and to do everything in its time.

Organizational Skills. The typical middle-class career now takes place in a bureaucratized organization. Even the professions, which used to be the stronghold of the individual practitioner, increasingly center their activities in an organization rather than a professional office. The doctor spends most of his time in and is most responsive to the social controls of the bureaucratically-organized hospital, rather than centering his practice in his own office. The recruit to the middle-class occupational world requires, if he is to operate successfully in it, the ability to get along in organization and bureaucracy. If the rules and constraints of large organizations frighten or anger him, he will not be able to achieve what he wants nor will he be an effective member of the organization. Among the specific things an effective member of a large organization must know and be able to do we can include the following: He must be willing and able to take the consequences for his own actions, to see ahead far enough to realize the effect of his actions on others and the organization. He must have some skill in manipulating other people, in getting them to do what he wants without the use of force or coercion; he must learn to be persuasive. He must have the ability to compromise, to give up some of what he wants in order to gain the rest; he must not be a narrow-minded fanatic, who either has his way or has none at all. And he must, finally, be knowledgeable and skillful in manipulating the rules and impersonal procedures of bureaucratic organizations to his own advantage, rather than being stymied and buffaloed by them.

The network of extracurricular organizations characteristic of the large state university provides a perfect setting in which to learn these skills. The student can participate in student politics, either as an active candidate or as a behind-the-scenes organizer. He can become an officer of one of the organizations that helps run campus activities. He can work on the student newspaper. He may be an officer of his fraternity or dormitory. A large number of students have experiences in one or more such organizations during their four years in college.

Melville Dalton, tracing the antecedents of successful industrial managerial careers, argues that experience in extracurricular campus life is a perfect background for success in industry:

> Taking a part in campus politics gives the student an experience he may not get outside of college, at his age, short of entering professional politics. He tries his hand at helping select and elect officers, and may himself serve, His part in the intra- and inter-organizational struggles is educational. He learns to move in and out of cliques and organizations with minimum friction. . . .
>
> He becomes sensitive to intangibles, and learns to live with the elusive and ambiguous. This unofficial training teaches him to get in his own claims and gracefully escape those of others that he must. He learns to appear sophisticated and to adjust quickly to endless new situations and personalities.[3]

Our observations at the University of Kansas corroborate Dalton's findings. Let me point out some additional sources of experience, important for the recruit to the middle-class occupational world, which Dalton does not mention. Many officers of campus organizations find themselves exercising responsibility for large amounts of money; they may administer budgets running as high as $50,000 a year. Some of them administer programs of activity in which it is necessary to coordinate the efforts of several hundred or more of their fellow students. You have only to think, for an example, of the effort and organization necessary for the traditional Homecoming Weekend at any big university. Some students even have the experience of discovering that the important people with whom they come in contact have feet of clay. As they deal with officers of the university in the course of their organizational work, they may be asked to do things

3 Melville Dalton, *Men Who Manage: Fusions of Feeling and Theory in Administration* (New York: John Wiley & Sons, Inc., 1959), pp. 166–167.

they regard as improper. A typical case, which occurs in many universities, arises when some university officer attempts to prevent the student newspaper from publishing matter he believes harmful to the university. The student reporters and editors discover, in such a situation, that university officials are, after all, only human too; it is a shocking and educational discovery for a nineteen-year-old to make.

Motivation. The recruit to the middle-class world must, finally, learn to attach his own desires to the requirements of the organizations he joins. He must learn to have what we might call *institutional motivation.*[4] He must learn to want things simply and only because the institution in which he participates says these are the things to want. This linking of personal and institutional desire occurs in a paradigmatic way in college. The student learns that he requires, at the least, a degree and that he must do whatever it is the college asks of him in order to get that degree. This attachment to the long-range goal furnishes him with the motivation to continue in classes that bore or confound him, to meet requirements that seem to him foolish or childish. The college student learns to want to surmount the obstacles posed for him by the college, simply because the college has put them there. He learns to regard mastery of these external obstacles as marks of his own ability and maturity and, because he interprets the obstacles that way, sees his success in college as a sign of his own personal worth. The ability to link institutional and personal desires is probably an important prerequisite for occupational success in adult life.

I have just alluded to the major process by which the prospective recruit to the middle-class occupational world acquires the skills he does in college. In large part through participation in the college community, the student comes to define himself as the kind of person who ought to have these skills. He pins his self-respect and his sense of personal worth on acquiring them. He feels that he will have

[4] The sociological theory of motivation employed here is explicated in C. Wright Mills, "Situated Actions and Vocabularies of Motive," in Irving Louis Horowitz, ed., *Power, Politics and People: The Collected Essays of C. Wright Mills* (New York: Oxford University Press, 1963), pp. 439–452.

properly become an adult only when he has all these qualities and skills. He directs his effort and organizes his life in such a way as to achieve them and thus prove to himself and others that he has grown up.

Those Who Do Not Go to College: The Lower Class

Our problem is somewhat more complicated in considering the lower class, for two reasons. First, we know much less about lower-class youth than we do about those who go to college. Second, the lower classes must be divided into those who are mobile or potentially mobile — those who want to become middle-class, who share the aspirations of those born to the middle class — and those who are not. We can simplify our problem somewhat by leaving the mobile members of the lower class out of consideration, assuming that they need the same things the person born into the middle class does. We can assume further that at least some of them will get to college and with luck will have the same kind of experiences as the middle-class youth and achieve the same things. These assumptions, of course, are questionable and conceal many important and interesting problems. I make them only so that we can leave these problems in abeyance and turn to the more clear-cut case of the nonmobile lower-class youth who does not go to college. What does he need to know? Where does he learn it, if he does learn it?

We realize immediately that we do not know what constitutes the definition of maturity or growing up in the lower class. We do not know what goal of adulthood motivates lower-class youth — what they are striving for and what they see as the signs of successfully moving into the adult age-grade.

Since we have little solid data to go on, I have had to approach the problem in a roundabout way. There are many studies available of occupations into which lower-class youth move. By looking at these studies, I am able to speculate about the possible demands on the lower-class youth as he moves into the work world. I will compare the demands for skills and knowledge likely to be made on the lower-class youth with those made on the middle-class youth. In some respects, the demands are similar while in others, of course, they are quite different. I will then go on to consider the institutions in which lower-class youth may or may not receive the kind of education they need.

Lower-class youth move around a good deal, though probably not as much as middle-class youth. Insofar as they move less, they need less the training in independence from kin and community the college provides for the middle-class youth. In addition, other institutions may give them this training prior to their entrance into the work world. In particular, a hitch in the armed services may be functionally equivalent in this respect to college, though no doubt more traumatic. Similarly, since work and family tend to be kept quite separate from one another in the lower class, the need for elaborate training in getting along with the opposite sex and in poise in social situations is clearly not so important for the lower-class youth. It makes little difference in his adjustment to the adult world whether he knows which fork to use or not, whether he knows how to introduce himself to people or not. The training the college youth receives in these social skills does not come to the lower-class youth, but then he does not need it very much.

Clearly, any lower-class youth will be better off for having some marketable skills than otherwise. It cannot hurt him to know something for which there is a demand, something for which the demand is expressed in a good salary. You are better off if you know how to weld or run an IBM machine than if you do not; you are better off to know how to set hair or type and take shorthand than not. The desire for technical training among lower-class youth (reflected in their patronage of the trade schools that abound in any urban area) indicates that members of the lower class recognize this fact and are willing to do something about it. The substantial number of lower-class recruits to such subprofessional specialties as practical nursing testifies to the same thing.

It is not so clear, however, that lower-class youth need the qualities of sticking with the job until it is done or the ability to budget their time and energy wisely. Insofar as his work tends to be relatively simply organized, consisting of one or a few tasks rather than a large number, the lower-class young adult will have little problem allocating his time and energy. His job ends when the whistle blows at the end of the day, rather than spilling over into after-work hours as does the work of the young professional person or businessman. Nor, since his work consists of a number of tasks of relatively short duration, need he have the ability to stick to a job that lasts over a long time until it is done. No doubt it is a good thing to have these skills, no matter what kind of work you do, but some kinds of work are so organized as to make them necessary and to reward those who have them and punish those who do not, while other kinds of work are not so organized. The work of lower-class adults puts no great premium on getting things done and there is no good reason why members of the lower class cannot do without these skills. They do not need the training provided the middle-class youth by his experiences with the college curriculum.

When we come to the skills of manipulating other people so they will act in ways you want them to and of manipulating the rules and regulations of bureaucratic organizations, whatever the career aspirations of the lower-class youth, it is clear that these are important skills for him to have. Whether in the world of work or in other areas of their lives, members of the lower class constantly bump up against the world of impersonal bureaucracy. Their failure to understand it, how it works, and how its workings may be turned to their advantage, may cost them dearly. Herbert Gans, discussing the world of the Italian residents of the West End of Boston, notes some of the characteristics of their culture which made it difficult or impossible for them to deal effectively with government when their area was slated to be torn up for urban redevelopment.

Gans describes the West Enders as lacking in the skills of, indeed being characterologically unsuited for, the kind of interpersonal manipulation necessary for effective social action. They feared that anyone who attempted to lead them in any collective action was only out for himself and were afraid to follow him. Would-be leaders had no skill in coercing support; they were unable to overcome the fear of others that their interest was self-interest. Similarly, the world of impersonal bureaucracy was a mystery. They interpreted it in ways that made it impossible to act effectively. Gans speaks of

> . . . the West Ender's inability to recognize the existence of object-oriented bureaucracies. The idea that individual officials follow rules and regulations based not on personal morality but on the concept of efficiency, order, administrative hierarchy, and the like, is difficult to accept. For example,

when the redevelopment agency initiated its procedures for taking title to the West End properties and for relocating people and demolishing houses, West Enders refused to believe that these procedures were based on local and Federal regulations. They saw them only as individuals, and individually motivated, acts. Taking title to the land was described as a land grab to benefit the redeveloper. Relocation was explained in terms of the desire of the redeveloper and his governmental partners to push West Enders out of their homes as quickly as possible, so that the new buildings could be put up. The protest of redevelopment officials that they were only following standard operating procedures went unheeded.[5]

An extreme example of the kind of trouble a lower-class person can get into because he does not understand the workings of bureaucracy is furnished in the story told by Rocky Graziano of his war with the United States Army. Graziano, inducted into the army, refuses to get up in the morning, make his bed, or do any of the other things required of recruits. Since he is stronger and tougher than the people giving him orders, he sees no reason why he should obey them. Finally, he is taken to see the captain, who tells him that he is going to be taught a lesson and have some of the New York knocked out of him.

> So I said, "Listen, you bum, you may be a captain and all that, but you don't impress me so hot. If you think you're tough, come on outside and I'll fight you."
>
> "Soldier, are you crazy?" he says.
>
> "Maybe I'm crazy, but at least I ain't yellow," I say. Maybe that will draw the son-of-a-bitch outside.
>
> He made a quick move out of his chair. My instinct tells me he's coming at me right there in the office. I hauled back and let him have a good fast right on the jaw. Baroom! He crashes back across his desk, slides off the corner of the desk and onto the floor. I guess he was only reaching for the phone to call the MPs to come and get me. Well, my mistake.[6]

Naturally, Graziano ended up in the stockade and eventually in Fort Leavenworth. Middle-class boys may not have liked the army any better than Graziano did, but they knew enough about its workings to avoid his kind of trouble with it.

[5] Herbert J. Gans, *The Urban Villagers: Group and Class in the Life of Italian-Americans* (New York: The Free Press of Glencoe, 1962), p. 165.

[6] Rocky Graziano (with Rowland Barber), *Somebody Up There Likes Me* (New York: Pocket Books, Inc., 1956), p. 187.

The inability of members of the lower class to manipulate people and organizations undoubtedly costs them dearly, and in many other ways than the two I have just given examples of. In their run-ins with police, landlords, unions, factories, and retail merchants, their inability to understand the workings of an impersonal institutional order is an expensive luxury.[7] Their inability to manipulate people so that they can cooperate in the achievement of some common goal makes it difficult for them to fight against the people and agencies who exploit and harm them. It may well be one of the chief sources of difficulty in "making out" in life.

Insofar as lower-class youth do want technical training, because of the increased income it will bring, their lack of motivation is a serious weakness. I do not mean that they lack the desire to get the training, but rather that they lack the focus on long-range goals that will give them the push necessary to get through a course of technical training. Obviously, I overstate the case here, because many lower-class youth do finish such programs of training. But they are, perhaps, less vulnerable to the implanting of institutional motivation. Or it may be that the institutions in which they participate are not capable of implanting such motivation.

Lower-class youth do need to learn that their actions have consequences and that they are responsible for those consequences. In many kinds of lower-class work, the man who is unwilling or unable to understand and accept the consequences of what he does may be penalized. For instance, Ray Gold has shown that even the occupant of such a lowly position as janitor has serious responsibilities which he cannot take lightly. In sorting the garbage put out by his tenants, he discovers a good many of their secrets: he knows, for instance, which tenants are not paying their bills, by finding unopened letters in the garbage, and he has the responsibility of keeping this information to himself. Similarly, if he fails to take proper care of the mechanical equipment in a building, he may flood the building or cause the boiler to blow up, with resulting damage to life and property. Janitors come to take these responsibilities very seriously.[8]

7 *See* David Caplovitz, *The Poor Pay More* (New York: The Free Press of Glencoe, 1963).

8 Ray Gold, "Janitors Versus Tenants: A Status-Income Dilemma," *American Journal of Sociology*, Vol. 57 (March 1952), pp. 486–493.

In the same way, the young man who becomes a dance musician learns that he must take seriously the contracts he makes, even though these are made in an offhand verbal way. If he fails to show up for a job he has contracted to play, he will find himself in serious trouble with the band leader and the union as well as the employer. The young man who has not learned to take this kind of responsibility seriously, who does not recognize that his failures will have undesirable consequences, can find himself in a great deal of trouble.[9]

I have till now ignored the question of whether there are skills other than those desirable for life in the middle class which the lower-class person needs to learn. I have ignored it largely because I do not know the answer to it. We can speculate, however, that the conditions of lower-class life may be different enough from those of middle-class life that there are such necessary skills. For instance, physical violence is much more common in lower-class areas and families than it is in the middle class. The lower-class person certainly needs to know either how to avoid violence when it occurs or how to handle it. In the same way, lower-class occupations tend to be much more responsive to general economic conditions. Therefore, the lower-class person faces a chancier economic prospect and must be prepared to put up with violent fluctuations in income. His life is more unstable.

We can also raise the question of whether learning some middle-class skills may not be a disadvantage for many aspects of lower-class life. To have learned to take seriously certain kinds of middle-class manners and styles of dress and speech would seriously unsuit one for many kinds of factory and office work.

The Institutions of Lower-Class Education: Trade Schools and Others

A great variety of institutions exists to give training to lower-class youth. They include trade schools of many kinds (secretarial, technical, and so on), subprofessional training programs (as for practical nurses, masseuses, and medical and dental technicians), apprentice-

[9] *See* Howard S. Becker, *Outsiders: Studies in the Sociology of Deviance* (New York: The Free Press of Glencoe, 1963), pp. 101–119.

ships such as are found in many unionized trades, in-service training programs, schools in the armed forces, and, finally, the experiences of those who simply go to work in a small shop or factory and acquire a set of skills in what is not nominally an educational institution.

I have argued that what lower-class youth most need to get from their educational experiences is, on the one hand, some set of salable skills and, on the other hand, the ability to recognize and reckon with the consequences of their actions. It might also be that these educational experiences could help with other problems, such as meeting an appropriate mate. How are these educational organizations set up? What can they teach? What are the problems of education in such circumstances? Again, I do not know the answers to these questions. We are now in the process of planning a study of precisely these kinds of educational organizations. In the meantime, I can only speculate about what is likely to be true about them. In what follows, I will speak mainly of the trade school and not consider the somewhat different problems of apprenticeships and the other varieties of educational institutions just mentioned.

An immediately apparent fact about trade schools is that they tend to be one-sex schools. Just as the occupational world is divided into those jobs considered proper for men and those considered proper for women, so the trade school (unlike the college, which offers a generalized training for many kinds of jobs) is ordinarily limited to one or the other sex. Men go to welding school; women go to secretarial school. Men study to be tree surgeons; women study to be airline hostesses. The trade school offers none of the vast opportunity for mingling casually with members of the opposite sex that the residential college does. The maturity achieved in the area of relations with the opposite sex by those who do not go to college is achieved outside the confines of any educational institution.

Typically, too, the trade school does not have the vast network of extracurricular organizations that characterizes the residential college. There is no equivalent training ground in which the youngster who does not go to college can get experience in dealing with the world of organizations. There are no offices for him to hold, no responsibilities for him to exercise, no political situations in which he can learn to maneuver and can acquire the kind of flexibility

Dalton speaks of. Whatever experience of this kind the person who does not go to college acquires, he gets somewhere else than in school.

Whatever the noncollege youth learns in a trade school, then, he learns in the encounter with his teachers. Presumably, he acquires those skills the school is set up to teach. But does he also have the experience, characteristically undergone by the college students, of having to learn something in order to earn some future reward? The college student, as I have said, has institutional motivation. He may not care about chemistry, history, or English literature, but he does care about passing his courses successfully, because he wants to graduate. He wants to graduate because the degree will open many doors, both occupational and social, for him in the world he moves into.

But what can the person who goes to a trade school expect as a consequence of learning what the school has to offer? First of all, he can probably expect something much more limited than the college student. The training he gets will open only a few doors, will get him a job in the specialty he is trained in, but no more. Conversely, he does not stand to lose very much if he does not do well. If he does not graduate from welding school he won't be able to be a welder, but he will still be able to do a great many other things, for failure in welding school makes no record that will harm him in any other area. Therefore, it is likely that the trade school student is interested in his studies only insofar as he expects what he learns to be useful. The apparatus of courses and requirements which gives structure and organization to the life of the college student does not exist for him. He may not even care very much whether he continues or not. The educational institutions themselves provide none of the reinforcement and support for continuing along the line of educational activity he has begun that is provided for the college student.

There is one important exception to this. Many schools prepare a person for state-required examinations necessary for a license to practice a trade. The person who studies to be a masseuse or beauty operator, for instance, must pass an examination set by a state board. This can provide some motivation for continuing in the course even though the student finds it dull. Nevertheless, as I have said, if he fails or drops out he loses nothing but the tuition already invested.

This being the case, the trade school student probably does not have the experience the college student does of having to meet a set of requirements in order to achieve some desired consequence. He does not have to "meet his responsibilities" as the college student does and does not have that kind of experience which we have seen is undoubtedly useful even in lower-class work and community life.

On the other hand, precisely because he is interested in the subject matter and not in more abstract goals, the trade school student may have a problem not characteristically faced by college students. He may be concerned, because he is interested mainly in the utility of the knowledge he is getting, about getting the maximum amount of knowledge out of his teacher. When we consider that trade schools are profit-making organizations, it seems a possibility that teachers tend to string out the presentation of substantive material so as to spread it over a longer period of time and get more tuition.

What student culture there is in trade schools and similar places remains to be discovered. It may well be, however, that the common problem most students in them have to face is precisely the problem of forcing the teacher to teach them more than he wants to. (Interestingly, we found this same kind of perspective among medical students, who felt that teachers were holding back on "practical" knowledge.[10] And indeed they were, since they considered "practical" knowledge to be worthless unless one understood its theoretical basis. The perspective of trying to get the teacher to "give" more may, perhaps, arise whenever the student is greatly concerned with knowing enough in a particular area after he gets out of school.)[11]

Conclusion

Though this paper was written to be presented at a conference on the role of the library in solving urban social problems, my readers

10 *See* Howard S. Becker, Blanche Geer, Everett C. Hughes, and Anselm L. Strauss, *Boys in White: Student Culture in Medical School* (Chicago: University of Chicago Press, 1961), *passim.*

11 Since this paper was written, the study of trade schools (mentioned earlier as being in the planning stage) has come into being. It is being conducted jointly by myself and Blanche Geer of Syracuse University, with financial support from the National Institute of Mental Health. It is still too early in our research to know whether and to what degree the speculations presented in this paper are correct.

may have remarked that I have not as yet even mentioned the library. This struck me, too, as odd, if not embarrassing, and I tried, when I had gotten this far in my writing, to think why it might be so. It seemed to me, after some thought, that the reason I had not mentioned the library was because it was very likely that the library had no role to play in solving the problem of how noncollege youth are to achieve maturity.

If the kinds of education available to those of our youth who do not go to college are not adequate to teach them the things they will need to know as adults, some institutions will have to take up the slack if the problem is to be solved. It may be that new institutions will be needed: the Peace Corps or the projected Domestic Peace Corps, for instance. The growing interest in providing technical training of new kinds, as in the mental health field, might lead to the development of new and more adequate educational institutions. Or older institutions — the armed services, conventional schools, libraries — might adapt themselves in some way.

But not all institutions are equally suited to solving all problems; each has facilities that fit it for dealing with some things better than others. Nevertheless, it seems that our great public institutions — of which the library is one — feel a compulsion to do *something* about every problem that comes to be defined as involving the public welfare. Whether it is the unwed mother or the hydrogen bomb that claims our attention, the great public institution feels that it ought to be taking a hand in things.

It may well be that such large multipurpose institutions as the public library are equipped to deal with many kinds of problems. Still, given limited resources, the library probably ought to confine itself to those problems it can best deal with. Further, librarians might do well to recognize that there are some problems they cannot deal with without transforming the library into a quite different kind of institution than it at present is. The lesson of my analysis of the problems of noncollege youth may be precisely that this is one of a perhaps large class of problems which require for their solution kinds of action for which the library is not equipped and which might best be left to other institutions better able to handle them.

PART II

FUNCTIONS OF LIBRARIES

HERBERT J. GANS

*THE PUBLIC LIBRARY IN PERSPECTIVE**

The planner views the public library as an institution that should achieve publicly desirable goals and should be planned so as to achieve these goals with a maximum number of desirable consequences, a minimum of undesirable ones, and at the lowest possible cost.

A major difficulty in selecting goals has been the two conflicting conceptions of the library: the *supplier-oriented,* arguing that the library should achieve the educational and cultural goals of the librarian; and the *user-oriented,* arguing that the library should cater to the needs and demands of its users. The library usually upholds the supplier-oriented concepts in its professional literature, and adopts the user-oriented conception in actual practice, if only to get its budget approved.

Philip Ennis argues for a supplier-oriented conception; a library that does not merely respond to public demands and publisher trends and that must develop a priority ranking of goals on the joint basis of its own community's needs and its community power structure.[1] Frank Riessman argues for a library that is "a place for consumption — for use — rather than a highly organized storehouse of

* Some of the material in this paper is taken from "A Comprehensive Planning Study of the Public Library," an unpublished monograph prepared in 1955 under a grant from the Russell Sage Foundation at the Institute for Urban Studies, University of Pennsylvania.

1 Philip Ennis, "The Library Consumer," p. 31 of present volume.

culture," although the consumers with whom he is concerned are at present not users of the library.[2]

Following are six current views of the goals and functions of the library, including one of my own which I believe will best meet the needs of the library in a changing metropolis. The first two are supplier-oriented, and the remainder are user-oriented.

The first alternative sees the library as a reservoir of culture, a storehouse of significant books. This is a traditional concept, recently revived in the American Library Association's proposal for regional libraries that in the city, would mediate between the central and the branch library. The emphasis is on the quality of the collection, with less concern for the needs or demands of the actual users.

The second alternative, also a historic one, sees the library as an educational institution. It will motivate people to read — convert them from nonreaders to readers, so to speak — and help those already reading to shift from "ephemeral" to quality books. Although this idea lingers on in the goal statements of the library profession, it has not received much support from those who pay the bills or from library users. If Berelson's 1949 analysis of library use is still valid — and I think it is — the library has not attracted education seekers other than children who use it as a homework aid.[3] Since users come voluntarily, the library must attract those people who are motivated already, largely of the middle-class and better-educated sectors of our population, or those in search of recreational reading. These users demand little educational material and they ask few educational questions of the reference librarian. They probably learn a great deal from their recreational reading, although this has not been considered in the empirical research of library use and reading. Moreover, few librarians are trained as educators or have the time to educate their clients. Also, television and teaching machines are in many ways better educational devices — especially for the functionally illiterate — than the books and periodicals which are the library's stock in trade.

2 Frank Riessman, "Low-Income Culture and the Urban Library," paper presented to the Symposium on Library Functions in the Changing Metropolis, Dedham, Massachusetts, May 1963.

3 Bernard Berelson, with Lester Asheim, *The Library's Public* (New York: Columbia University Press, 1949).

These institutional conceptions of the library are highly regarded by the profession, but they are less desirable from the point of view of community planning. If a library is not attractive to many users, it is difficult to demand for it a large share of scarce public resources. A library that is not used sufficiently is a waste of resources, even if its goals are noble and the size and quality of the collection are outstanding. Consequently, the library must be user-oriented; it must be planned to attract enough users to justify public expenditures. It is doubtful whether a library system designed to attract primarily high-brow users would be in the public interest; these users generally have access to a university library or can afford their own books. The question is, which users should be planned for?

One user-oriented alternative is to plan the library for all users, which Ennis describes as the cafeteria. This was the practice before the age of the paperback, when libraries supplied recreational reading to the middle-class population, in addition to serving children and students. The paperback has cut sharply into fiction circulation, and Ennis is right in questioning this type of library.

A second user-oriented approach is to plan for people who are not being served adequately by bookstores, book clubs, paperbacks, or university libraries. This is the practice of many libraries today that are catering to the sharply rising numbers of children and students and also to a more slowly rising number of readers of nonfiction of the best-seller variety as the old adult audience for fiction is disappearing. This is a desirable solution. The library need not compete with the paperback book, especially the low-priced one. Not only is a drugstore more accessible than the public library, but also the average reader may freely indulge his taste for entertainment and fantasy without feeling guilty about his choice of leisure reading. Best sellers are available in paperback almost as quickly as they are in most public libraries. Moreover, paperbacks are cheap, and need not be returned. For those who can afford them, they represent a reasonable source of leisure reading. Conversely, children and students either cannot afford books, do not wish to buy them, or simply cannot get them as cheaply and efficiently as adults can get their books at the corner drugstore. They and people who want nonfiction reading of the non-best-seller sort will be dependent on library service until paperback publishers meet their demands.

A third user-oriented alternative is for libraries to serve a distinct clientele efficiently. This is what Ennis suggests when he excoriates the library for following public demands and the output of the publishing industry. His solution, to determine community needs and the wishes of the community power structure, is too general. Also, the community power structure should not determine the characteristics of the public library, because its members may have neither the interest nor the ability to understand the library and its users. Moreover, they sometimes exercise religious censorship and racial discrimination.

The final alternative draws on some of the above conceptions, and includes Ennis' idea that "each public library must make its own priority ranking." It is based on two assumptions. First, the library should supply mainly those not served adequately by other methods. Second, it ought to serve those who live near it, for studies compiled by Berelson have shown that most libraries serve people living within one-half to one mile away, or to put it another way, that most people will just not go much further to borrow a book. This is probably still true in today's cities and, with corrections for car and bicycle use, in the suburbs as well. It is even valid for the main library, as studies show that a large proportion of its users come from areas closest to it. Furthermore, this datum is a major reason for the success of the drugstore paperback rack, for the drugstore is often more accessible than the library. Population dispersion over the metropolitan area has not hurt the library so much as the ability of the paperback publishers to bring their wares close to the reader.

The fact that the library can only attract people within a relatively small radius means that it has no other alternative but to serve whoever lives — or works — in that radius. Since most people get their books where they live, rather than where they work, the library is basically a neighborhood institution, and the most important part of the system is the branch library, that modest, unassuming structure that often gets so little recognition or status from librarians. The main library may be the flagship of the system, and its large collection and monumental architecture the pride and joy of the community boosters, but it is the branch library where people come to get their reading materials.

If the concept of the library as serving those within its service area is combined with the principle that it ought to cater principally to those people not served by other methods of book distribution, some more detailed comments can be made about library planning.

First, libraries will have to be planned for the kinds of people who live in its service area. In middle-class neighborhoods the contemporary library is desirable, with its emphasis on child, student, and nonfiction readers. These people can afford hardbacks or paperbacks for recreational reading, and can accept the middle-class aura that surrounds the public library.

In low-income areas, which are increasingly important in the changing metropolis, this middle-class library is unsatisfactory. Here a library is needed that invites rather than rejects the poorly educated person, with book stock, staff, and catalogue system that are designed to help him read. It should be geared to two types of readers: the small number who are already motivated, and may even have the middle-class values and skills that are prerequisite to using the library and, more important, the much larger number of people who cannot afford paperbacks and who would like to read but are afraid or scornful of the ethos of the middle-class library. There is a third group of potential users here, adults who cannot read well but would like to learn. The library should teach these people or work with adult education agencies that could teach reading. The publishing industry might pass paperback overstock or slightly damaged books to libraries in low-income neighborhoods. These books would be freely distributed in order to encourage reading and develop potential buyers. Most important, as Riessman points out, the library must be a permissive, inviting place to the low-income population that is now so numerous in the American city.

In areas populated largely by older people, the library might provide more reading rooms, stocked with newspapers and magazines as well as books. Here lonely people could come to read and to converse in a kind of informal community center, perhaps in a storefront that would provide companionship as well as reading.

In suburban areas, the library is predominantly a children's library, and should be geared to the needs, the noise level, and the attention span of the youthful population.

Conversely, in business districts the library serves people with special informational needs, and there the branch would be — as in many cities — stocked with nonfiction and reference material for those who work there. In suburban industrial areas, such a public library might have to be on wheels.

The diversity of plans required to meet the needs of a small service area might overwhelm a library planner. But this fear is groundless, as ecological research has shown; neighborhoods are much the same the nation over, and fall into recognizable types. From these, several corresponding library plans could be developed, patterned for the urban middle-class residents, older people, suburban middle-class areas, low-income areas, and business districts. Using consumer research in the specified neighborhood, the appropriate type of branch library could then be adapted.

If the branch is the major component of the library system, what is the role of the main library? It ought to be the reservoir of the high-quality collection and of infrequently used materials. A central staff of highly trained reference librarians could serve the entire metropolitan area through closed circuit television. This main library should ideally be modeled on a metropolitan main library like that of New York City, although in most cities such a facility is out of the question. There, local university or college libraries can be connected administratively to the public library to serve the specialized research and scholarly users and functions. Although the reference staff and some of the book stock of the main library must be located centrally, both to the city and the suburbs, less demanded books could be stored in a low rent district from where they could be shipped easily — and quickly — to either the main or a branch library.

This conception of the public library in the changing metropolis is only one among several possibilities. It is biased toward a user-oriented conception of the public library, yet it is also traditional in viewing the library as a book-centered institution, rather than as a communication-centered one. Traditionalism is in turn based on two assumptions: first, that the public library ought to serve readers rather than data-retrievers; and second, that it is difficult to divert institutions from their traditional ways, which makes it more desirable to develop new institutions for new needs. This approach to library planning is based on the idea that existing institutions not only should perform effectively their original functions but also should be adapted to the changing needs of their communities.

NATHAN GLAZER

*THE LIBRARY IN THE COMMUNITY**

I have been asked to discuss the changing urban community and the public library. About the first I know a certain amount and have thought a good deal; about the second I know almost nothing — or rather, I know only what a public library user of thirty-five years may know of public libraries. As a result, what I have to say may be in part grossly in error, and in part terribly naive. Nevertheless, I responded because I saw an opportunity for the public library to help the new emerging texture of our country, and an opportunity for (conceivably) the knowledge of the very rapidly changing pattern of American life to be helpful to librarians.

Thirty-five years ago, when I first took out a library card in the Carnegie branch on East 96th Street in New York City, American cities were still highly concentrated. They depended largely on public transport, and their suburbs were relatively limited in extent and inhabited by well-to-do people. The small towns of this country, while stable in size or losing population, were still definable towns — the flood of urban expansion had not reached and swallowed many of them. There was a higher proportion of farmers — and they were further removed from urban influences. Radio had ended its first decade, but television was still a dream. The supermarket had not yet been invented, and the shopping center did not exist.

These references to the past have not been casual, for each of these things has had drastic consequences for the character of American

* This paper was delivered as an address to librarians in 1959.

urban life, and indeed American life in general. There are today three times as many cars as there were in 1930, and public transport has been in a state of crisis for twenty years. Urban physical expansion has covered vast areas, because a new pattern of living, based on the car, has thinned out the population. The concentrated centers of cities are in decay — losing retail business to new outlying shopping centers, losing middle-class and upper-middle-class residents to new outlying suburbs, and yet despite these losses suffering from incredible congestion as the private automobile replaces public transportation. The small towns of this country, if they grow, do so only in their capacity as the outlying parts of growing metropolitan areas. In effect, the dream of decentralization held by early city planners like Ebenezer Howard and pressed by men like Lewis Mumford is coming to pass. The concentrated city areas are breaking up, and a loose semiurban texture spreads over the countryside.

All this is familiar. But what may it have to do with the public library? I am not sure of all of its consequences, but various thoughts have ocurred to me. To begin with, let us consider again the library of thirty-five years ago in a city such as New York. People visited it on foot. Since one is never so mobile as on foot, it was possible to visit it casually. Since it served a dense and concentrated area, it could be immobile — it was easily accessible, and the "bookmobile" was in its infancy, if indeed it had been invented at all. Serving a large population, the branch library could be remarkably well equipped. One could find in it major reference works that I think few local libraries today would have — Shepherd's historical atlas, the Cambridge modern, medieval, and ancient histories.

But more important considerations affected the relationship between the library and the urban community. For what was the urban community of 1930? It reflected still that great age of immigration that had transformed American cities and the American population. It was deeply affected by the American dream of upward movement, movement toward better jobs and higher incomes open to all. In an age in which the primacy of books as a means of communication and instruction had only recently been challenged by magazines, movies, and radio, the library had a certain awe-inspiring character. It was the repository of ancient wisdom, as well as of modern instruction, both of which might help people advance themselves. Its architecture reflected its higher position: solid, gray, granitic. The books themselves were soberly bound in maroon or blue, and dust jackets were not to be seen in public libraries — at any rate, in the libraries I went to thirty-five years ago.

I speak of the library in urban areas, and particularly urban areas influenced by immigration (as were most in America). In rural areas library services barely existed. In small towns, relatively unaffected by foreign immigration, a similar significance was attached to the library. There too the library was the place for young people who wished to improve themselves. There too the library, even if it did not have the architectural grandeur of the city library, tended to be in a solid building, perhaps the former home of some wealthy man or given by some philanthropist. I think of Richardson's library in Quincy, Massachusetts, and of the Forbes Library in Northampton — there are many others.

Let me refer to another characteristic of those days in contrast to our own: it is my impression that a higher proportion of the national income, whether it came from private philanthropists, foundations, or communities, was then used for libraries. It is hard for me to envisage today the kind of investment that produced the New York Public Library — the collection and the building — and the Carnegie branches. We are a richer society, but for various reasons we seem to spend less on certain kinds of public investments, or perhaps we spend them in different ways and different places. We spend for universities and parkways, rather than for libraries and city parks. The decline of the city park is of course yet another sign of the decline of the concentrated city; and the rise of the university a sign of the rise of bureaucratized and formal means of upward mobility, as against the less organized pattern of mobility by self-directed efforts which favored the first free libraries for young clerks or workers and was still evident in the New York libraries of the thirties.

If we now shift back to the contemporary situation, we find that many things have affected the position of the library. Some of these factors have nothing to do with the changing city. One is the growing efficiency of publishing in making more and more books available cheaply, and in finding more and more ingenious means of distribution of books. But this development is aided by new urban patterns — for example, the new supermarkets have become one of the chief vehicles for the distribution of children's books and paperbacks. Another is the growing prosperity that makes it possible for people to buy these cheap books. A third is the continued development of mass circulation magazines on fairly high levels of sophistication — the kind of thing *Life* does. A fourth is the enormous impact of television as a time-consumer. A fifth is the steady decline of the Horatio Alger pattern, among both the children of immigrants and the young people of small towns. By the Horatio Alger pattern I mean the notion of self-advancement through self-directed learning and reading; and its replacement by steady upward steps on a bureaucratic ladder, whether in education or in the bureaucracies of business and government. Thus we have institutional libraries rather than public libraries. A sixth is the growing efficiency of institutions that take up some part of the traditional library's roles — particularly the schools, now equipped with their own libraries. When I went to the public elementary and high schools of New York, there were no school libraries — or if there were no one knew about them and no one used them. The pattern of book borrowing was confined to the public library.

And finally there is the impact of the change in urban texture itself, the spreading of the population such that it is impossible for more and more Americans to get to any place by foot or on public transport. Let us consider in this complicated matter of the change in urban texture one factor — the shift to cars. Now the shift to cars, it would appear to me, must have serious consequences for libraries. For one thing, the most frequent users of libraries — their natural markets, so to speak — are the young — children, adolescents, and teenagers, who have more time to read, who have less money to buy magazines and paperbacks or to patronize lending libraries, who do not have access to institutional libraries, and who also are still able to browse because their interests are unformulated. This audience, it would appear to me, must be seriously affected by the fact that the library is less accessible as the community spreads out. Now the library cannot spread as the community spreads. It declines rapidly in usefulness as the number of items it contains declines. A library, to be of any use, must be of a minimum size. The community can spread out; the library cannot, except through the relatively unsatisfactory means of bookmobiles, or smaller branches, or a system of borrowing from central depositories. Useful as this pattern of a library network is, it is the best way of killing potential bookworms — bookworms must browse, and the man who wants one book and just that one and can wait patiently for it to come from some central depository is not, I submit, the best customer of a municipal library.

The central point about the library in the era of diluted urban texture is that it cannot easily serve as a browsing point, as a refuge. It can become a service, and it can be as efficient as a service as it ever was — supplying specific books, specific information, and the like. However, the library was once more than a service. It was an institution of a peculiar sort, created not only by its special services but also by its physical existence (the kind of building it was), the kind of people who staffed it, the kind of people who used it, and the special hush it created.

Up to this point I have said little that cannot be placed under the heading "nostalgia for the 96th Street Carnegie Branch." I have referred to negative consequences for libraries of recent developments; and yet librarians are much better trained to give service today, the area of services has greatly expanded, and so on. The fact is that the library is a noisier and busier place, and what is the point of emphasizing subtle qualities that have disappeared or are disappearing?

The point is this: there is something in the old-style library which should arouse more than nostalgia, and that could do a great deal for this contemporary American urban texture, with its never-ending stream of cars, its hardly varying pattern of single-family houses, its busy supermarkets and shopping centers. The library can emphatically *not* be part of the shopping center, hardly differing in its bright, glassy architecture and its brightly dust-jacketed latest best sellers from the other stores and the supermarkets.

I have referred to the hush of an old-style library: it is just this hush that the new urban texture of America needs, and that our efficiency in merchandising has pretty much wiped out. Even the churches — or at any rate the up-to-date churches — ring with the noise of play, meetings, lectures, discussions.

David Riesman once referred to the hard-cover man who needs a hard-cover book. I would now refer to the hard-cover library, in which one is protected by columns and stones and heavy wooden paneling and heavy wooden bookcases and signs of "QUIET." In such a library the important thing is the setting for a special kind of experience — being alone with a book, or with a lot of books — and not the efficiency of the librarian, or the art exhibit, or the lecture-discussions (though if the cover is hard enough, and the institution large enough, there is no reason why these things cannot go on at the same time). In the new American urban texture there is no place to hide, or, more positively put, no place to be alone in a productive and restorative way. Back yards and front yards merge into a common open lawn; countryside is less accessible; stores assault every sense. Even the new texture of the dense city, in both its public housing or its upper-income urban renewal area, tends to eliminate central courts or enclosed areas. I would be very unhappy to see the library lose this function in an effort to be more popular and to attract more people by means similar to those used by other institutions, commercial and public.

I have spoken of the special atmosphere of a library. Now it is true the atmosphere of the old Carnegie branch was in part based on the awe of the immigrant and the unlettered for a distant and higher culture associated with higher status. In a society where wealth is ever more accessible, where the paperback format strips the mystery from even the most esoteric books, where the quality of awe is less and less in evidence — whether in response to the socially prominent or the old or the politically great, or in response to the things of the past — is there any point in dwelling on this feature, and saying the library should try to retain something of this quality? Let me say that this quality of awe was itself an important aspect of the structure of traditional concentrated cities. Monuments were meant to create awe, as were government buildings, and the houses of the rich. I think one of the reasons the new urban texture is so boring is because of its flatness. The triumph of democracy has meant that neither the schools nor the government buildings nor the houses of the rich any longer sharply distinguish themselves from the prevailing building style. I think the talk of monumentality in architecture that is so common today indicates that human beings want this variety and complexity in their environment, and regret that the monuments of today, if any, so often look like factories. The library was traditionally that building that was closest to being a monument — often used in its negative connotation as a relatively dull thing, for it could be a purely passive collection of books, open to inspection at given hours. But it is this sense of monumentality that is so lacking in contemporary life. And since in any case the primary function of the library is passive — simply to hold onto the records of civilization, and to hold onto them whether anyone wants to use them or not — it is well suited to restore fully this aspect of monumentality to urban texture.

The need to serve is admirable. But the need to serve also creates certain distortions: for example, in its drive for efficiency and usefulness it tends to ignore the importance of the inefficient and the unusable — the book that is rarely or never borrowed (but if it is of value it will be someday), or the space that merely exists as space, with the wonderful psychological effect space can have. Think of the entry into the main catalog room of the New York Public Library, and its exhilarating effect. Certainly a new library would arrange the trays more efficiently, rather than around the sides of a great room, with consequent loss of a kind of experience which is rapidly becoming rarer in society, and for which I feel the need — and for which others I think also feel the need.

There are other things I could say — for example, that contemporary urban texture needs accent points to break its unending and unvarying forms, and that institutions such as libraries, rather than blending in inconspicuously — as another store, another little factory, or another modern house — should emphatically try to be an accent. They should look different — and serve as markers, points where the eye may rest, givers of names to neighborhoods and streets. And here the space outside the library is also important, and I don't mean the parking areas. The library must try to create even for a small stretch outside it the kind of peace that it should try to create inside. Once again, I think of the space around the New York

Public Library — inefficient but certainly not unused, as anyone can testify who has been there at lunch time, and used, too, in ways harmonious with what a library is for. It is not a place for loud talk and bustle.

I am afraid much of what I have said will be dismissed as pointless conservatism. Let me indicate that I am not a conservative. While I look at the past with some regrets, as who does not, I feel positively about the civilization that is emerging and may emerge in the United States. But the emergence of this civilization needs continuing criticism, and a subtle criticism, for as obvious defects are overcome less obvious ones emerge. I see the need for certain kinds of qualities in modern urban life. I see that certain institutions are peculiarly suited to add these qualities — museums, universities, government buildings, churches, indeed all the buildings that do not exist or need not exist for immediate and efficient use and profit. Among these institutions is the library. Its role in the city, as something special and distinctive, creating a unique quality, is one that we cannot afford to lose.

RICHARD L. MEIER

THE LIBRARY: AN INSTRUMENT FOR METROPOLITAN COMMUNICATIONS

Sometimes, when investigators get together, the paths of their respective researches join up. The shared experience enables them to advance beyond past conjectures and thereby achieve a vision of potentials far grander than they were capable of comprehending only a short time earlier. Because they are pioneers in the acquisition of knowledge it is quite possible that this vision of order in the immediate universe is the first that has been seen by anyone. These occasions of collective insight are high points in the life of an investigator. They are part of what John R. Platt has recently called the "excitement of science."[1]

Some years ago in Cleveland I participated in such a meeting of minds. The operations research experience with creating more efficient institutions was matched against my own work on the organization of cities. The outcome of this conjunction of interests is perhaps typical of the fate of ideas that are so inspired.

The operations research group at Case Institute of Technology that is led by Russell J. Ackoff had been consulting with firms and branches of the government. They collected information about internal operations and performance which would assist in systematizing functions and procedures. The findings were incorporated into explicit recommendations for reorganization and reform. They had, for

1 John R. Platt, *The Excitement of Science* (Cambridge, Mass.: Houghton Mifflin Company, 1962).

example, just completed an extensive analysis of the communications behavior of scientists, including the way they draw upon the scientific literature, which led to suggestions for the organization of research laboratories and the establishment of suitable information retrieval systems.[2]

The Case Institute of Technology as a unit, and the operations research group in particular — since it filled the role of an active reform-oriented goal as well as a source of expertise — had been rethinking its relationship to the neighborhood and the metropolitan area. An institution for research and higher education, particularly if it is not supported from taxes, should be a pacemaker and a leader within the urban milieu. Therefore the operations researchers began to connect Case's function as a supplier of documented knowledge with the outcomes of their recommendations to their clients. Always, it appeared, some of their recommendations were intended to lead to a rationalization of the communications systems and information processing. The organization was expected to accumulate more knowledge about its economic and scientific environment, and this knowledge was to be drawn upon for various allocation and programming decisions. Therefore information storage requirements were built up both inside and outside the organization being advised. The need for increasing contacts between a repository of knowledge and the users in the region was quite obvious to them.

My own studies had started from the impact of modern science and technology upon society, but they quickly focused upon the problems posed by urban growth. A very good case could be made for the assertion that cities are being reconstructed so as to facilitate a steady expansion of public communications.[3] For example, urban traffic analysis suggests that the automobile became extraordinarily popular not because of dollars-and-cents savings that it could promote or because of an illusion of power that it conveyed to the driver, although both arguments are important for small minorities of the automo-

2 This work is summarized in the article by Miles W. Martin and Russell J. Ackoff, "The Dissemination and Use of Recorded Scientific Information," *Management Science*, Vol. 9 (1963), pp. 322–337.

3 Richard L. Meier, *A Communications Theory of Urban Growth* (Cambridge, Mass.: Massachusetts Institute of Technology Press, 1962).

bile-operating population, but because it was tremendously convenient for expediting face-to-face meetings and man-to-nature interactions.

These face-to-face contacts are exceedingly important for the organization of the city. They promote trustful relations between people, and out of repeated associations new projects are born. A vigorous city boils up new associations of individuals, new project proposals, and a continuous flux in its institutions as they adjust to the changes of the social environment. A large share of the projects have commercial objectives, but many in the area of professional activity and community affairs arise from a mutually felt inner sense of obligation. The projects are tied together into programs that are undertaken by existing institutions, or they may result in small independent enterprises, some for profit but mostly for fun.

Economic logic tells us that, lacking surprising major discoveries of new natural resources, the accumulation of knowledge must precede increases in output. The knowledge can lead to the refinement of technology and an improvement in organization. The rate of increase in this knowledge and its utilization exceeds the growth rate of gross national product in the United States both in value and in absolute quantities.[4] One can state the same proposition with a slightly different emphasis: *Improvements in the level of living of urban societies depend upon the substitution of information for natural resource inputs.* Thus we in the School of Natural Resources must expect that the results we obtain in our researches will contribute to declining expenditures upon resource development in society! We expect to persist because resources are scarce, but only in the shadow of an expanding library and information-processing service.

What we saw together, the operations researchers and myself, was a metropolitan integration of the stockpiles of knowledge with the communications systems which conduct messages from one part of the city to another — the telephone network, the mail, the courier services attached to the telegraph or parcel delivery organizations, and even the possibilities inherent in closed circuit television — so that the distribution costs for knowledge would be greatly reduced

4 Fritz Machlup, *The Production and Distribution of Knowledge* (Princeton: Princeton University Press, 1962).

despite the increasing complexity of information retrieval. The im-improved accessibility of information in the schools, businesses, and laboratories should induce people living within reach of these services — the urbanites — to save time and energy by drawing upon the reserves of expertise and recorded information.

Stocks of Information

Systems theorists think in analogs and express themselves in models. Our vision of the city was compounded of analogies with various familiar information-rich contexts. We were particularly aware of those functions that are undergoing rationalization, and of these the best known are those that are components of the financial system.

The library is very much like a bank. A library contains accounts of refined, recorded experience of quite general value that have been accumulated over a long period; similarly, a bank is a repository of savings accumulated over an equivalent length of time. The bank must keep an important portion of its resources in a liquid state, so that cash for the demand deposits can be obtained upon very short notice; a library keeps much of its information at its fingertips in order to meet the kinds of requests that are to some extent predictable; the working files of most utilities and large corporations are similarly organized. Much of the remaining assets of a bank require specialized intermediaries, referred to as brokers, who can usually liquidate these securities in a matter of hours or days. The library equivalent to the broker is the reference librarian. One can continue in this fashion and identify a series of equally persuasive parallels, but it is highly significant that in most towns and cities in the United States the library is now responsible for a larger number of small loan transactions than any other local agency. There are more books being formally lent than small sums of ready cash, hand tools, or automobiles.

Control of money has quite a few advantages over control of the stocks of print. Thus it is not surprising that banks can find funds for rationalizing themselves earlier than libraries. Banks have chosen to evolve a system for coping with their accounts with speed and an absolute minimum of error. Quite a few have effected a computerization of their operations that is compatible with other banks and the remaining manual operations in their own organization. It is not worth while elaborating the technology of the system and the structure of the resulting network of flows, because in detail it differs markedly from what is needed to solve the library problem. It is better, instead, to look forward to a day, perhaps a decade or so hence, when it would be economical to construct a documentation system for a metropolis that is as physically integrated as the banking system is now becoming.

In this case one can imagine several collection points for data and documentation in a metropolitan area. One of them would receive data about the working of the urban services in the city itself that might normally be made public if there were room in the newspapers and the annual reports. The public institutions presently generate tremendous amounts of information in the course of administration, much of which could be made available to the public. This includes educational data, traffic statistics, land use maps, judicial processes, recreational programs, health information, retail sales trends, cultural resources, etc. The city would have much more detailed private information concerning individuals, their organizations, and their property that should not be released, but the impersonal aggregated data can be used by the specialists for identifying trends in the metropolis to which many must adjust and therefore should be kept public. The prospect is for the metropolis or megalopolis to assemble the information for its own decision-making needs, and then make available those portions of it which are likely to be of general value. The constellation of cities in the Los Angeles area, for example, plan to spend tens of millions of dollars per year in this way within a few years, and perhaps hundreds of millions thereafter, so that the resultant municipal data "bank" should build up very rapidly to significant dimensions.

Another such center would assemble the new materials in science, technology, and literature from the world at large. The research laboratories and the staff assistants in the executive offices are willing to pay considerable amounts of money for comprehensive coverage that is also readily accessible. Technical education and higher education can also be very considerably assisted. The rapid access features are likely to be used also for enriching certain features of secondary education that are linked to current affairs and modern science.

For both such institutions the systems analyst and the systems engineer can sketch some advanced designs. These two mechanized compilations of information would undoubtedly draw heavily from each other when responding to complex requests. But there is much information that is valuable, yet inconvenient to store and retrieve by mechanical means. Much of this material is already found in a metropolitan library system. In the future we may expect that the routine and high-volume demands now made upon a library would gradually be divested from it, while the unique services to adult education and scholarship would be expanded. Despite the proposals now being put forth for automating certain library procedures, it appears that the labor of acquisitions, cataloguing, and bibliography compilation would render the library an unsuitable locale for their application. Labor-saving devices will continue to be added, but automation rarely.

Information-Demanding Tasks

The rapidly increasing outlay for higher education and the still more rapid increases in the graduate schools are evidence of a profound shift in American society. More than 90 per cent of the new college graduates and very nearly 100 per cent of the M.A.'s and Ph.D.'s will be settling in metropolitan areas. They have learned, for the most part, how to use documentary source materials and are likely to put these skills to work if it is at all convenient. A smaller number from the most advanced colleges and universities have been learning how to use a "data bank." The availability of new data stimulates a more frequent "review of the past record" in a search for hypotheses that explain trends in recently assembled information, so the increase in information results in increased use of the library for serious (as contrasted to recreational) purposes. Thus the logic of numbers compels us to forecast unprecedented demands for the use of library materials. Metropolitan areas of middle rank are likely to be only a decade behind the leaders in the growth of demand.

The changes in educational institutions are providing a basis for anticipating the transformation of the metropolitan areas. The large universities with better-than-average libraries, including state universities and the metropolitan part-time study oriented institutions such as New York University, Boston University, and Roosevelt University, are expanding to meet the enlarged demand for education, while the prestige centers and private colleges expand very slowly. Therefore the expanded output naturally becomes competent in the vast, anonymous environment typical of the metropolis, while the graduate of the small college (who does not go into graduate school and learn how to adapt there) will feel more comfortable in the far suburbs and exurbs. Thus the trends in the growth of educational institutions are creating a built-in bias in the metropolis that encourages a much heavier use of recorded information on a per capita basis than exists at the present.

These potentials exist as pent-up demand unless the quality of information service is vastly improved. When strong pressures for information exist, any small improvement in accessibility will result in a markedly greater expenditure of time and effort for acquiring information. A typical situation is as follows: At present it will be discovered that a half an hour of search and delay is encountered for each half hour of time spent reading the materials that are found. A significant reduction of the time required for the preliminaries results within a year or two in the reading of twice as much material with the expenditure of fifteen minutes on search and delays. Thus in an hour and a quarter twice as much information is extracted from the stockpile of knowledge as was previously obtained in an hour. An economist would say that the demand for knowledge is highly elastic, so that a decline in costs (time is more important than money in this case) results in a much larger increase in utilization.

Each new metropolitan problem can now be conceived in information requirement terms. For example, only a decade or two ago the rise in juvenile delinquency and the continuing dropout from high schools would have been formulated as a problem in counseling and law enforcement. Now multipronged programs are being fitted together which allow this part of the population a few extra inexpensive mistakes as they are being guided toward niches in blue-collar and white-collar society. The process requires the training and retraining of perhaps five times as many professionals and subprofessionals in a much wider range of specialties. The new guidance and training personnel must know about each other's expertise. The coordination of action requires much reading that goes beyond what is available in textbooks and is only found in reproduced materials and articles. The juveniles arming for white-collar jobs are also impelled to "look up things." Therefore, the success of the program now depends heavily upon access to literature in as many as twenty different specialized areas of expertise and upon hundreds of kinds of subject matter. The materials around which artistic expression is developed, musical records, the reproductions of drawings and paintings, and films, are increasingly combined with contemporary fiction, and this task would increase the demand for a convenient stock of such materials.

Implications of Larger Information Flows

The data banks, libraries, and documentation centers need to be linked together by a network of channels, so that each can draw upon the other and the clients can obtain access according to the urgency that the occasion demands. Simple extensions of the telephone and telegraph network are already available, while for maps and other illustrated matter it may be anticipated that easier-generated beams of light will be well suited to metropolitan communications. The major production plants in the region, the research and development laboratories, the colleges and universities, the high schools and training centers, the executive offices, and the centers of public information would need connections with increasing capacity. The flow rates of information in American cities are increasing approximately five per cent per capita per year but, as has already been emphasized, a new and convenient facility is likely to bring about a surge of growth quite a bit larger than that for a few years.

The growth of a communications network has properties which mislead many observers. Educated people, in particular, believe that new channels and new media should stimulate serious communication and cultural materials that are in good taste. Popular institutions, such as public communications systems, cannot operate so as to satisfy the taste of the elite. The public must learn by doing, and the intellectuals will manage to stay far enough ahead of the masses to decry their taste.

Most communications systems are justified on the basis of the value of the crucial messages. The requirements of the decision systems establish how much fidelity is needed for transmitting at peak periods. The rest of the time is filled in with routine, casual, playful, or experimental messages, depending upon who has access to the channel.

The principle is perhaps easiest to understand when it is applied to international military communications that can be intercepted but not decoded. Then it is necessary to fill in the non-message-sending time with random noise and relatively trivial messages. Otherwise other nations would be able to detect well in advance every major recommitment of forces or other shift in plans merely by noting the changes in the volume or rate of message sending. One need only remember a generation or more ago when the stock market ticker was relayed manually by expert telegraphers, and the traders could tell the pace of the buying and selling by judging how fast the reports were being relayed. Any excitement on the floor would be communicated by the telegrapher merely by speeding up the pace of dit-dotting to a rate just short of confusion. The military must disguise what the business community has come to depend upon. Various items in the news, gossip on the exchange, and even salacious jokes came over the wire when trading had halted.

Yet the filling of the channels with trivia allows experimentation with expositional techniques, exploration of the potentials of effect, the discovery of clichés, the development of fads, and the differentiation of a variety of publics with identifiably different tastes. With a greater repertory of images, skilled senders, and experienced receivers, it is possible to communicate more about the challenges to the metropolitan society, and obtain more adequate responses. The recreational use of libraries and other media when they became more accessible is a reflection of the need to grope and explore, leading eventually to the organization of a more adaptive society.

The adaptive metropolitan society that has learned to use these greatly expanded sources of information, and the communications channels leading into them, will develop highly specialized tasks among the sender group. The receivers learn to find material and programming that are interesting to themselves. These improved capacities are no different fundamentally from those that are expected to be obtained from education. Education, too, represents an accumulation of socially approved knowledge that has been acquired through communications channels.

The Importance of Hierarchy

Libraries in large cities tend to decentralize their services with branches, bookmobiles, and lending programs for school systems. They are even now setting up telephone reference services and making special arrangements for the local industries and research laboratories. They handle the overflow from colleges and universities. The ability to provide service has been assisted by the siphoning off of the less sophisticated inquiries at the neighborhood and institutional level.[5]

The information collection for the metropolitan data bank tends to have its roots in the respective neighborhood offices, special bureaus, and local institutions. The peak of the pyramid, the summit of the hierarchy, is the information on regional shifts. It serves people who are solving production or distribution problems that do not exceed the regional scale. National and international questions are barely significant in most cases.

The documentation center that seems to be a necessary component in this *troika* has quite a different structure. It collects information of worldwide scope and universal generality. That material is made available with a minimum of delay to the technologist and scientist.

[5] K. G. Harris, "Metropolitan Reference Services: Patterns, Problems, Solutions," *Library Journal*, Vol. 88 (April 15, 1963), pp. 1606–1611. In Detroit 60 per cent of the library users are students, more college there than most places elsewhere. Various large city libraries report 20–60 per cent patronage from suburban addresses.

It seems inevitable that this institution cannot very readily be created independently in various metropolitan centers. Communications channels are now becoming cheap enough so that the principal centers can be limited to a handful in the world, and the metropolitan relay stations would best be used to assemble from local document collections the most frequently requested materials. The obvious candidate for such a centralized service is the U.S. Library of Congress.

The cataloguing of the expanding flow of published matter operates as one of the principal deterrents to regional centers. The cataloguing, as with abstracting and indexing, must be a highly coordinated and centralized function, otherwise the service will quickly be overwhelmed by the rising flood of literature. The Library of Congress has already taken the initiative in cataloguing and has even begun to consider "its potential role in the study of metropolitan library problems and in the support given industry by public and university libraries."[6] It has also been studying the mechanized retrieval systems. Not much progress can be made, however, unless there is increased financial support at the national (or international) level.

The restrictions imposed by the copyright laws and traditions must be treated separately. I have assumed that an equitable solution can be found, analogous to the compromise worked out for musical compositions used by mass media.

In conclusion, it must be admitted that the original vision of an integrated information system for a metropolitan area ws faulty. It seemed then that the initiative lay within a few decision centers in a forward-looking metropolis, and that a sum of money amounting to only a few dollars per head would be sufficient to install a complete system. Most of the new services could be tied in with the telephone accounting system, as with telegrams and flowers, and they would pay for themselves.

The mistake lay in the documentation system for technology and science. The initiative there must be at another plane. Then the metropolitan area contains merely a branch of an international net-

[6] F. H. Wagman, "Toward Understanding of the Library of Congress," *American Library Association Bulletin,* April 1963, p. 322.

work which links stocks of knowledge that are collected or generated locally. It seems likely now that the rapidly increasing sophistication of space science and technology, oceanography, meterology, and nuclear energy will drag both the natural and behavioral sciences with them. The cost of organizing the information is small as compared to the total investments anticipated in this field, and the potential savings are remarkably large.[7]

Thus I suspect that one of the most significant "fallouts" from space science developments for urban society in the modern world is the stimulus it must give to information systems at the national and international level. This is the area I must study in order to discover how my dream of much more perfectly informed urban settlements with the highest cultural attainments could come to pass. Space research not only instigates demands for greater accessibility to data and past experience, but may also provide us with the technology for the communications channels that link up the various subcenters of a metropolis and the various metropoles in a world order.

[7] The present status of information retrieval in the United States borders on scandal. Attempts have been made to design and construct sophisticated retrieval systems, even though the coding schemes permit only 60 to 70 per cent retrieval. Mechanical systems have thus far turned out to be several times more expensive than manual methods, but this is a function of scale of operations. Once a large demand exists, and congestion in the documentation center becomes a significant source of delay and error, it seems likely that a mechanized retrieval system will be more economical than manual systems. Thus a national system should be justifiable on the basis of cost long before any regional system. R. R. Shaw, "Information Retrieval," *Science,* Vol. 140 (1963), pp. 606–609.

CHARLES M. TIEBOUT AND ROBERT J. WILLIS

THE PUBLIC NATURE OF LIBRARIES

One of the most important issues on the minds of those concerned with libraries is the failure of the public to support adequate library services. We suggest that the main reason for this is the public's failure to understand the library's function in the modern metropolis. Our discussion, cast within the newly developing concepts of public finance, will suggest that this is probably correct, but for the wrong reasons. In fact, we want to explore the possibility that part of the problem is that librarians may misunderstand the economic nature of library functions.

The Public Nature of Libraries

The economist views the public library as one of a number of goods and services, both public and private, which compete for the consumer's dollar vote. Let us start the analysis with this basic question: why is a library public rather than private? One list of library functions would include circulation of books, general reference, reader guidance, adult education, group services, browsing, and business-industrial reference service. All of these are parts of the library function of making information available,[1] subject to budget restraints and the relative importance given each function. If this is what the library does, we want to see why this is a public function.

1 As suggested in Gerald W. Johnson, "Role of the Public Library," *Public Library Service* (Co-ordinating Committee on Revision of Public Library Standards, Public Libraries Division, Amercian Library Association, Chicago: 1956, pp. vii–xiii), page xi.

For, if it is public, it can be expected to have characteristics similar to other public goods and services.

Government at its various levels provides goods and services such as public protection, national defense, highways, postal service, schools, and hydroelectric power. Some of them, such as police protection and national defense, are known as *social or collective use goods,* partly because no one can be excluded (within the geographic area affected) from benefiting from them whether they pay for them or not. If private enterprise should attempt to provide such a social good, each individual would tend to understate his preference for such a good because, if others purchase it, he will also share in the benefits without any cost to himself. Since everyone benefits, everyone in the affected area should pay, hence government through taxation provides the good.

The functions of the public library do not fit this characteristic of a social good. Clearly, the consumer could be excluded from the benefits of library facilities and services. This suggests that the libraries could be private enterprises; and, in fact, the original libraries in the United States were provided privately, charging fees for their use.

Another aspect of social goods is shown by the case in which short-run costs are zero. A good example of this is a bridge. Assuming it is not used to capacity and that maintenance costs because of use are nil, the cost of one extra car using the bridge is zero. Any fee which keeps someone from using the bridge will be a misallocation of resources; therefore, from the viewpoint of social welfare, there should be no charge for crossing the bridge.

The circulation function of the library may come close to fitting this "bridge-type" classification. With a large number of books and baring the case in which more than one person wants the same book at the same time, the cost of one extra book being circulated is close to zero. The same may hold true for the reference function, although probably not for facilities and library staff devoted to reference aid.

While this may provide a rationale for public ownership, it hardly seems enough. As with a bridge, those who do not pay can be excluded from enjoying the benefits. Further, although the costs of additional reference and circulation functions are close to zero, this is not true in the long run. Somehow these costs must be met. In a market economy, the principle of "those who benefit should pay" seem justified. In turn, user fees seem appropriate. A public library, therefore, must have as its rationale that there are benefits not revealed by the ordinary processes of the market.

The Externalities of Library Functions

Another way of looking at social goods such as national defense is in terms of externalities. In John Dewey's parlance, there is a third-party effect in the exchange between two individuals. Economists label these third-party effects "externalities." Simply stated, externalities imply a spillover of benefits or harm to persons not directly involved in the transaction. In the national defense example, consumption by one person does not cut down consumption by another. How does this apply to libraries?

One argument used by librarians is that the benefits of libraries accrue to the community as a whole. While the person who actually uses the library is the main beneficiary, others benefit as well. The terms "better citizen" and "more educated community" describe this social benefit. In part, this is also the justification for subsidizing higher education. The problem is precisely this, that the benefits of libraries do accrue to both users and nonusers. Why this is a problem can be seen if we assume we know more than we actually do.

Suppose the benefits of a library accrue 60 per cent to the individual user, and the external benefits accrue 30 per cent to the local community and 10 per cent to the nation as a whole. Most likely we would want to charge 60 per cent of the cost to the individual and pay 30 and 10 per cent out of local and federal taxes respectively. This would provide some sort of equity. Even though the library benefits more people than the individual user, the problem is solved. Yet, before looking into the implications of this kind of solution, we must recognize a somewhat different type of externality.

It is thought that libraries provide a merit good. A merit good is a product or service which could be provided by the market, but is not demanded in sufficient quantities according to a value judgment made by society. One such good might be fluoridated water, which can be obtained in the market but is deemed meritorious by some communities so that it is provided free to all water users and paid for by a general tax. In effect, what society is saying by such a program is that individuals do not realize how much they benefit from fluoridation as well as society does; i.e., that fluoridation is good for people. In economic terms, such judgments by society interfere with consumer sovereignty on the grounds that if people knew the extent to which they would benefit from using or avoiding such goods, they would be willing to purchase in the private market an amount equal to what society deems necessary. But, since tastes can change, inducement or coercion must be used to obtain an optimal solution.

The public library, analyzed both historically and functionally, would seem to be primarily a case of a merit good. Oliver Garceau quotes from the charter of a social (subscription) library in Castine, Maine, which was founded in the 1820's.

> It is greatly to be lamented that excellent abilities are not infrequently doomed to obscurity by reason of poverty, the *rich* purchase almost everything but books; and that reading has become so unfashionable an amusement in what we are pleased to call this enlightened age and country.
>
> To remedy these evils; to excite a fondness for books; to afford the most rational and profitable amusement; to prevent illness and immorality; and to promote the diffusion of useful knowledge, purity, and virtue at an expense which small pecuniary abilities can afford, we are induced to associate . . .[2]

Social libraries, however, were not the solution. Garceau goes on to note that ". . . subsequent evidence has clearly shown that fees, no matter how small, do prevent wide use of the library."[3] In fact, when no fees are charged, one survey has shown that only 18 per cent of the population uses libraries at all; the top 10 per cent of these make 71 per cent of all visits to the libraries. Yet 75 per cent of the population wants libraries.[4] Evidently, 75 per cent of society seems willing to subsidize the 1.8 per cent of society which dominates

2 Oliver Garceau, *The Public Library in the Political Process* (New York: Columbia University Press, 1949), pp. 18–19.

3 *Ibid.*, p. 19.

4 *Ibid.*, p. 137. Garceau cites Survey Research Center, "The Public Library and the People," Ann Arbor, Michigan: mimeographed, 1949, p. 3.

the use of libraries, because they believe libraries are good for people — especially other people.

An analysis of library functions would also suggest their merit good justification. Reader guidance, adult education, group services, and even browsing are provided in an attempt to stimulate the virtues of reading and education. They are provided free because people would not pay a fee for them, yet they are good for people. If libraries are not considered merit goods, it is difficult to see why they should stock a few copies of best sellers when private lending libraries are willing to lend these at a small fee. But a library would be a very dull place without current and controversial books which attract people to the library initially. The hope is that they will use the other facilities and noncurrent titles after they have been introduced to the library.

If we agree that a library is good for the individual and therefore a merit good, the question arises, how should it be paid for? Clearly, it needs to be subsidized to reduce the charges to the individual. If this is not done, the utilization will be too low.

To summarize our discussion so far: we have argued that libraries are public for a variety of reasons. Most important in our view are the social goods characteristic of benefits beyond the user and the merit goods characteristic of good for the individual. Now we are in a position to see what this implies for the changing patterns in the metropolitan area.

Library Functions in the Changing Metropolitan Area

Suppose a library system is to be established *de novo* in a metropolitan area. Further assume a fiscal state where there are no problems of independent governmental units. How would a library system be arranged; or, barring an answer to that question, what variables would be considered?

On the cost or supply side, one would want to know the economies of scale for the various library functions. Given these and the patterns of spatial demands, library functions can be located efficiently.[5]

[5] Charles M. Tiebout, "An Economic Theory of Fiscal Decentralization," *Public Finances: Needs, Sources, and Utilization* (National Bureau of Economic Research. Princeton, N.J.: Princeton University Press, 1961).

Most likely the reference function will be located in a single building near commercial activities, perhaps by some kind of Weberian weight analogue solution.[6] Branch libraries can be established to meet demand and to satisfy scale economies. The point to be made in all of this is that we still need to determine to what degree the library system is a social good, to what degree it is a merit good, and to what degree it is a private good that should be subject to user charges.

Even in the good fiscal metropolitan area this is no simple task. To begin with, consider just the social benefits; they are not uniform throughout the area. A branch library on the north side may do little for the south side. This suggests the difficulty in accounting for social benefits. Somehow, through the political process, not the market, the degree of social benefit and also meritoriousness must be determined. Only when variables such as these are determined can we set up an efficient system.

What happens in the balkanized metropolitan area? Here the problems become acute. Industries which need the reference service may have moved out of the central area. The lower income minority groups who inhabit the gray belt around the central core may be those for whom the merit concept most applies. The independent suburb, on the other hand, may generate a relatively high per capita demand yet be constrained by a low budget. All this, we suspect, is familiar — albeit the terminology we use is different. What we are suggesting is a rather general problem in providing social and merit goods in balkanized metropolitan areas. Library functions may serve as a prime example.

The problem of the social goods aspect is this: social goods are no respecters of political boundaries. Benefits from one community spill over into others. Unfortunately, so do the harms. In terms of economies of scale and the scope of the benefits, the most efficient size and location for a particular library function may not — indeed, probably does not — coincide with any political or taxpaying unit.

When we turn to the merit aspect, an acute problem arises with balkanization. If libraries are "good" and should be subsidized, who is to pay the subsidy? Residents of suburbs may be willing to sub-

[6] A. Weber, *Theory of Location,* translated by G. J. Friedrich (Chicago: University of Chicago Press, 1928), pp. 79–96.

sidize their own residents, but not those of the gray belt in the central city. This is a general problem of merit goods provided by levels of government below the federal, and no obvious solutions are evident.[7]

If these social and merit aspects are the two broad problems libraries face, what are the possible solutions? A reorganization of governmental units in the metropolitan area hardly seems called for on this basis alone. A second approach would be a public awareness campaign to show the benefit of library functions. To the extent that present services are inadequate in spite of past campaigns, added efforts may *not* be fruitful. This brings us back to the hypothesis which we introduced at the beginning, that library service may be inadequate, but for a different reason.

In spite of the added complexities in providing library services brought about by the changing patterns in metropolitan areas, the nub of the problem lies elsewhere. Library services may be inadequate. The reason, however, is not primarily because the citizen is unaware of this and may be willing to pay his share. More likely, the reason is that too much of the benefit of library functions is passed off as social or meritorious and not enough of the benefit is assigned to the user. Simply stated, the user is not asked to pay his fair share.

For libraries, the implication of this view is that more consideration should be given to user charges. Instead of worrying about how to make the public more aware of social and merit benefits, it seems appropriate to recognize the user or private benefits and to develop methods of charging for these benefits. Library services may be inadequately provided not only because the nonusing public fails to appreciate their function, but also because the user is not charged enough.

It has commonly been held that any fee charged for library service will prevent a wide use of the library. This is true in the short run, but may not be the case in the long run.

Any fee charged for library service will probably initially reduce

[7] Charles M. Tiebout and David B. Houston, "Metropolitan Finance Reconsidered: Budget Functions and Multi-level Governments," *The Review of Economics and Statistics*, November 1962, pp. 412–417.

the number of library users, especially if the quality of library service remains the same. In the long run, however, revenues from fees can be used to improve the quality of library services, and this could eventually result in an increase in the number of users beyond the initial level.

Three variables would be important in determining the long-run effects of a fee for library service: the ability of the library to improve service with increased revenue, the positive response of library users to improved services, and the negative response of users to the imposition of a fee. Many of the basic operating costs of the library are covered by its governmental subsidy. Library authorities should be able in the long run to improve library services, e.g., as measured by the number of books purchased, by a proportion as great or greater than that the revenue from fees bears to the existing library budget. The long-run effect of the charging of a fee will depend on whether the library is ultimately able to induce an increase in library use through this improvement in services that is greater than the decrease in use occasioned by the charging of the fee.

In attempting to assess the impact of a fee on library use, one should remember that in the long run library services can improve by more than the amount permitted by the initial revenue provided by the fee. As library service improves through the utilization of that revenue, library use and hence library revenue increase, and this in turn can lead to greater improvements in service and use. The process can continue until library service is at such a high level that further improvements in it will not attract further users.

EDWARD C. BANFIELD

NEEDED: A PUBLIC PURPOSE

The public library has more users and more money today than ever before, but it lacks a purpose. It is trying to do some things that it probably cannot do, and it is doing others that it probably should not do. At the same time, it is neglecting what may be its real opportunities. What the library needs is, first, a purpose that is both in accord with the realities of present-day city life and implied by some general principles, and, second, a program that is imaginatively designed to carry its purpose into effect.

This paper will begin with a brief look at the principles justifying *public* action. (Why should a public body distribute reading matter and not, say, shoes?) In the light of these principles, it will then consider what the public library has been, what it is now, and what it ought to be.

Some General Principles

Economists offer several justifications for governmental intervention to set the demand for a commodity or good (in this case library service).[1] One justification exists when the good is of such a nature that it cannot be supplied to some consumers without at the same time being supplied to all — examples are national defense and air pollution control; in such cases, it is impossible for the distributor of the good to charge a price for it, since he cannot withhold it from

1 *See* Richard Musgrave, *The Theory of Public Finance* (New York: McGraw-Hill Book Company, 1959), Chapter 1.

anyone who refuses to pay the price. Therefore (apart from philanthropists) only the government, which through its tax power can coerce everyone into paying, is in a position to offer the service. Clearly this justification has no application to libraries.

Another justification — and one which presumably *does* apply to the library — exists when the public will benefit in some way if the consumer consumes more (or less) of the good than he would if the government did not concern itself in the matter. If my consumption of a good — my immunizing myself against disease or my sending my children to school, for example — confers benefits of some kind upon the community at large, the government ought, in the community's interest if not in mine, to see to it that I consume a proper amount of it. In order to encourage consumption of such "merit goods" (to use an economist's term), the government may employ subsidies.

That consumption of certain goods confers benefits upon the community does not automatically justify government subsidies, however. No doubt it is a good thing from a public standpoint that I eat well, have a safe roof over my head, and go to the doctor when I am sick. But if I am compos mentis and not indigent the chances are that I will look after these matters without any encouragement from the government. The public does not have to pay me to eat; I will do so both because I must in order to stay alive and because I enjoy eating.

Public intervention to set the demand does not necessarily involve public production or distribution of the good. The school board sets the demand for school books, but it does not hire authors to write them and it does not operate its own printing press. The Air Force sets the demand for planes but it does not manufacture them.

By the same token, that a good is produced or distributed under public auspices does not imply the necessity of a public subsidy for the people who consume it. The function of the government may in some instances be merely to make up for a deficiency in the private market by offering consumers a good which from the standpoint of the community they ought to have and which for some reason no private enterprise offers. If no one saw fit to go into the shoe business, the government would have to. But if it went into the shoe business it would not have to give shoes away, or sell them for less than the cost of manufacture.

The Nineteenth-Century Purpose

Let us now look at the public library of the past in the light of these principles. In the very beginning, libraries were private associations for the joint use of a facility that was too expensive for any but the well-off to own individually. Some state legislatures conferred on the associations certain corporate powers, including the power to tax their members provided that a two-thirds majority concurred. They did this on the grounds that benefits to the community at large would ensue — i.e., that library service satisfied a "merit want." "These libraries," Franklin remarks in his autobiography, "have improved the general conversation of Americans, made the common tradesmen and farmers as intelligent as most gentlemen from other countries, and perhaps have contributed in some degree to the stand so generally made throughout the colonies in defense of their privileges."

Later on the corporations thus created were made public and were supported in part by taxation of the whole public. This was about the middle of the last century, when bright and ambitious farm boys who had mastered the 3 R's but not much else were flocking to the cities to seek their fortunes. "Mechanics libraries" were established to afford these Horatio Alger characters opportunities to pick up by home study the small amount of technical knowledge that then existed. Such libraries were not supported in full by the public — philanthropists provided most of the support — but they were tax exempt and they enjoyed other advantages. There were good reasons for giving them these advantages: anything that encouraged self-improvement on the part of the "respectable poor" tended to increase the productivity and wealth of the community. Besides, to the Anglo-Saxon Protestant elite that ran the cities, self-improvement appeared good in and of itself.

It was not until near the turn of the century, however, that most sizable cities had public libraries in the present-day sense. There was no doubt about the public purpose of these libraries. They were to facilitate the assimilation of European immigrants to the urban, middle-class, American style of life.

The immigrants — many of them — were highly receptive to what the library offered. They came — many of them — from cultures that respected books and learning; with few exceptions they were eager to learn the language and customs of their new country and to get ahead in a material way. There was, accordingly, a high degree of harmony between the public purposes being sought through the library and the motives and aspirations of its potential clientele.

Times Have Changed

Today the situation is entirely different. The Horatio Alger characters and the immigrants have long since passed from the scene. There are, to be sure, more poor people in the large cities than ever (they are not as poor in absolute terms, however, and they constitute a smaller proportion of the metropolitan area's population), and the movement of the poor from backward rural areas of the South and Puerto Rico is likely to continue for some time to come. The present-day poor, however, represent a new and different problem. Their poverty consists not so much of a lack of income (although they lack that) as of a lack of the cultural standards and of the motivations, including the desire for self-improvement and for "getting ahead," that would make them more productive and hence better-paid. "The culturally deprived of today's cities are not on the bottom of a ladder; they do not even know that one exists," the editor of a bulletin for librarians has written in an article extremely opposite to the present discussion.[2] Many of the poor are "functionally illiterate," some though they have gone to, or even graduated from, high school. Giving them access to books will not accomplish anything.

Assimilating the lower class into the working and the middle classes may be a public purpose of the highest urgency. (Some people, of course, assert that lower class values — certain of them,

2 Kathleen Molz, "The Public Library: The People's University?" *The American Scholar*, Vol. 34, No. 1 (Winter 1964–1965), p. 100. The writer wishes to express his appreciation of Miss Molz' criticism of an earlier draft of this paper.

at any rate — are as worthy of respect as any others.) But however compelling the case for assimilation is thought to be, the question has to be faced whether the library is a fit instrument for the purpose.

Certainly no one believes that the library is now of any service to the lower class. By and large, libraries are of the middle class and for the middle class. With rare exceptions, librarians have the wrong skin color, the wrong style of dress and make-up, the wrong manner of speech, and the wrong values (among other things, they think that people should be quiet in the library!) to be acceptable to the lower class. The feeling is mutual, moreover, for most librarians are probably no freer of class and race prejudice than are other middle-class whites. The consequence is that the lower class is repelled by the library, or would be if it ever got near it.

A few library boards have tried to change this, but without much success. Some will say that their methods have not been sufficiently ingenious: they should establish store-front libraries and staff them with lower-class librarians, preferably radical ones; they should employ supersalesmen to go from door to door selling cheap reprints, and so on.

If one believes that lower-class adults can be enticed to read, there is much to be said for making this a primary purpose of the library and for trying any approach that offers the least promise. It may be, however, that the educational level of the lower class is so low and its demoralization so great that no efforts on the part of the library will have much effect. Something much more fundamental than library service may be needed — for example, compulsory nursery school attendance from the age of two or three.

Not being able or willing (or both) to serve the lower class, the public library has tended to make itself an adjunct of the school, especially of the middle-class school. Children have always been an important class of library users, but in recent years they have become the principal clientele of the public library in many places. Children sent by teachers to use books in connection with course assignments crowd some libraries after school hours to such an extent that adult users have to leave. (In certain Los Angeles schools, teachers require each pupil to borrow at least one book a week from the public library!) Here and there libraries have been forced by the sheer weight of the children's numbers to place limits on service to them.

One reason for this invasion is that, thanks to the "baby boom" of a few years ago (which, of course, is still continuing), there are more children than ever. Another is that the schools do not have adequate libraries of their own. (Two-thirds of all elementary schools have *no* central library, and those with central libraries have only five books per pupil in them on the average.) Still another reason is that it has become fashionable among teachers to require "research" papers (in some places third-graders swarm into the public library to do "research") and to assign, not a single textbook, but a list of readings, some in very short supply, selected by the teacher from a variety of sources.

Public libraries were not designed for large numbers of children and are usually not staffed to handle them. The wear and tear on books, librarians, and innocent bystanders is therefore very great. In Brooklyn, it was recently reported, book losses — not all of them caused by children — run to 10 per cent of the library budget. In some places rowdyism is a serious problem.

In fairness to both the children and the adults, the schools ought to have adequate libraries of their own; presumably they will have them if the aid-to-education legislation now pending in Congress is passed. Children should not be excluded from public libraries, however — it is a good thing for them to go now and then to a place the atmosphere of which is decidedly adult — but they should not be sent there to do assignments; they should go to the public library on their own initiative to find books that please them and in the expectation of entering a world that is not juvenile.

The Light Reader

Apart from school children, the most numerous class of library users consists of light readers, especially middle-class housewives. The books these readers borrow are not *all* light, of course, and even the ones that are light are not the very lightest; public librarians do not buy out-and-out trash. Nevertheless, a considerable part of the circulation is of romantic novels, westerns, detective stories, and books on how to repair leaky faucets, take off excess fat, and make money playing the stock market. About two-thirds of the books public libraries lend to adults are fiction, and most of these are probably light fiction. (Unfortunately, libraries do not use more relevant categories than "fiction" and "nonfiction" in their record keeping.)

It is hard to see how encouraging light reading can be regarded as a public purpose. That the housewife finds it convenient to get her detective story from a public rather than a rental library is certainly not a justification for the public library. Her neighbor, who may not care to borrow books and whose income may be less than hers, will be coerced into paying taxes to support a facility that is for her convenience. Why should he be? Whether she gets to sleep by reading a novel, by watching the late show, or by taking a sleeping pill — indeed, whether she gets to sleep at all — is a matter of indifference to him and to the community at large.

If it could be shown that light reading leads to serious reading, a justification for public action would exist. In the case of uneducated people who are introduced to books by the library, such a showing might possibly be made. But it is highly unlikely that it can be made in the case of the middle-class readers who constitute most of the adult library users. For the most part, light reading leads to nothing except more light reading.

Unless reason can be found for believing that light reading confers some benefit upon the community, the public library should leave the light reader to the rental library, the drugstore, and the supermarket. If for some reason these readers *must* be served by the public library, they should be charged the full cost of the service, including, of course, a fair share of the rental value of the library building and site. Charging the full cost of service would soon put the public library out of the light-reading business, but this would prove to be a benefit even from the standpoint of the light reader. He would find that when the public library stopped competing with rental libraries by giving its service free, they and other profit-making enterprises (the paperback counters of the drugstore and supermarket, for example) would fill the gap and give him better service than he got before. If there is a demand for thirty copies of

Peyton Place, the rental library makes haste to put that many on its shelves. The public library, not being under the stimulus of the profit motive and (let us hope) feeling itself under some obligation to serve more important purposes, buys only one or two copies of such a book if it buys any at all. This, of course, accounts for the more than 3,500 rental libraries (not to mention the drugstore and supermarket counters) that are competing successfully with the tax-supported libraries.

The Serious Reader

The proper business of the public library is with the *serious* reader and — assuming that the library cannot be an effective instrument for educating the lower class — with him alone. "Serious" reading is any that improves one's stock of knowledge, enlarges one's horizons, or improves one's values. Reasonable men will disagree as to where the boundary should be drawn between light and serious reading; that does not render the distinction invalid or useless, however, although it will lead to some practical difficulties.

The common-sense assumption is that all serious reading confers some benefit upon the community. This would be hard to demonstrate in a rigorous way (imagine trying to specify the amounts and kinds of benefits conferred upon various sectors of the community by, say, so many man-years of novel reading, so many of historical reading, and so on); but the difficulty, or impossibility, of demonstrating it does not mean that the assumption is wrong.

That an activity confers benefits upon the community does not, however (as was remarked above), constitute a sufficient justification for publicly supporting it. Perhaps those who read serious books would read as many of them if public libraries did not exist. (Indeed, conceivably they might read more of them, for if an existing institution did not stand in the way, a new and more effective one, public or private, might come into existence. Any foreigner who has observed the operation of the government salt and tobacco monopoly in Italy will agree that other and better ways of distributing these commodities are possible. To the Italian who has never been abroad, however, the idea of putting the government out of the salt and tobacco business might seem preposterous. "How then," he might ask, "could one possibly obtain these indispensable articles?") Most serious readers have adequate or more than adequate family incomes; it seems likely that if they had to pay the full cost of their reading they would not read less. If this is so, there is no reason for the public to subsidize their reading.

The relatively few serious readers who are poor — so poor that to pay for library service would entail a sacrifice of something else that is necessary to an adequate standard of living — present a problem. They could of course be given service at reduced rates or free. This is widely done by colleges, and there is no reason why there should not be "library scholarships" for all who need them. If such an arrangement involved use of an objectionable means test (would it be objectionable to give service free to all families with incomes of less than $5,000 if the user's statement that he belonged to that category were accepted without question?) or if the costs of record keeping were unduly high, the sensible thing would be to make the service — the standard service, not necessarily special services — free to all.

If it is decided that serious reading must be subsidized in order to secure for the community all of the benefits that it wants, it need not follow that the best thing for the library board to do is to own and circulate a collection of books. There may be much better ways of accomplishing the purpose. Perhaps, for example, those who have responsibility for allocating the library fund — let us now call it the "fund to encourage serious reading" — would get a greater return on the investment by inducing the local supermarket to display a big stock of quality paperbacks and to have one-cent sales of them now and then. Or, again, perhaps the fund would best be used to subsidize the rent of a dealer in used books who, because of the ravages of urban renewal or for other reasons, could not otherwise stay in business.

Some Illustrative Ideas

Assuming, however, that such radical innovations are out of the question and that the practical problem is to make some minor changes in the existing institution, what might be done?

Here are a few suggestions.

1. Provide soundproofed cubicles that readers may rent by the week or month and in which they may keep under lock and key books (subject to call, of course), a typewriter (rented, if that is what they want), and manuscripts. Nowadays few people have space at home for a study. Many libraries have reading rooms, but there are no places where one can read, let alone write, in privacy and comfort. (An habitual smoker, for example, cannot read if he is not permitted to smoke.) The New York Public Library at 42nd Street is probably the only public library with cubicles (they are supported by an endowment); there is a long waiting list for them.

2. Offer the services of a "personal shopper" to take orders by phone and to arrange home deliveries and pickups. Many readers are too busy to go to the library, especially when there is no more than an off-chance that the book they want is in. The personal shopper could also arrange fast interlibrary loans and for the photocopying of hard-to-get, out-of-print books. (Publishers naturally object to the copying of copyrighted material. But perhaps they could be persuaded to give libraries a general permission to make one copy per library of works that are not available for sale.) A fair number of the larger libraries have had "readers' advisers" ever since WPA days; the advisers' time is usually entirely taken up by children, however; in any case, only handicapped persons are assisted *in absentia.*

3. Buy a large enough stock of *serious* books so that no reader will have to wait more than, say, two weeks for a copy. Bentham's remark about justice can be paraphrased here: "Reading delayed is reading denied."

4. Display prominently, and review in library newsletters, those current books that are not widely reviewed by "middle-brow" journals. Many people suppose that all worthwhile books are listed, if not actually reviewed, by the better newspapers and magazines. This is not the case. Scholarly books are ignored as often as not; some of them are mentioned only in the academic journals, the names of which are unknown to most serious readers. The natural tendency of the library is to make a fuss about the very books that the ordinary reader would be most likely to hear of anyway. It should try instead to make up for the deficiencies of the commercial institutions by calling attention to the less-well-advertised books.

5. Maintain up-to-date, annotated bibliographies of the sort that would help introduce a layman to a specialized field. A physician, let us suppose, wants to know what social science has to say that is relevant to problems of medical organization. What books and journals should he look at first? If the library had a file of reading lists, course outlines, and syllabi used in colleges and universities, together with bibliographical notes and articles from academic journals, he could be assisted to make his way into the subject. A good many of the better libraries have materials of this sort — more materials, probably, than most of their serious readers realize. Even so, there is probably a good deal of room for improvement both in the quality of the materials that are collected and in the methods by which they are made known to library users.

6. Offer tutorial service for readers who want instruction or special assistance. Perhaps the physician would like to discuss his questions with a social scientist. The library might have a social scientist on its staff or it might bring one as a consultant from a nearby college or university. The tutor would be available for an hour's discussion or, at the other extreme, to give a short course.

7. Have a mail-order counter supplied with a directory of all books in print, a list of available government publications, and the catalogues of some dealers in used and hard-to-find books. A librarian should be on hand to help buyers find what they want. In the many towns and small cities that are without proper bookstores, this kind of service might go a long way toward making up for the lack.

The Library's Failure Is Typical

The library is by no means the only public institution that with passage of time has ceased to serve its original purpose and has not acquired a new one that can be justified on any general principles. Very likely it could be shown: (1) that the professionals most involved, and a fortiori everyone else, have given little serious thought to the nature of the purposes which presumably justify not only public libraries but also public parks, museums, schools, and renewal projects (to mention only a few activities of the sort that are in question): (2) that such purposes as might plausibly be advanced to justify such activities are ill-served, or not served at all, by the activities as presently conducted; (3) that these purposes could usually be better served by the market (rigged perhaps by public authorities) than by public ownership and operation; (4) that in most cases using the market would result in greater consumption of the good and in less waste in the supplying of it (public institutions tend to offer too much of those goods that are in light demand and not enough of those that are in heavy demand); and (5) that certain goods not offered by private institutions are not offered by public ones either, and this even though increased consumption of these goods would confer relatively large benefits upon the community at large.

To find the reasons for this state of affairs, one must look deep into the nature of our institutions and of our political culture. Organizations tend to perpetuate themselves and therefore to embrace whatever opportunities come along, however unrelated these may be to any previously-stated purposes. Public organizations, moreover, often exist as much to symbolize something as to accomplish something. These are only two of many considerations that doubtless should be taken into account.

DAN LACY

*THE DISSEMINATION OF PRINT**

It is the purpose of this paper to describe the characteristics of the book publishing and distributing industry in the United States, both as the producer of the principal body of materials used by libraries and as a complementary means of disseminating those materials to the residents of large cities. Because of their symbiotic relationship, the potentialities and limitations of publishing help to define those of the library system, and the reverse is equally true.

Book publishing has certain economic and technological characteristics that distinguish it from the other communications industries. These have been described in some detail in an article entitled "The Economics of Publishing" in the Winter 1963 issue of *Daedalus*. Some of these are:

1. The publishing of books, unlike broadcasting or the publication of newspapers, does not require the ownership of an expensive plant. With rare exceptions, book publishers do not manufacture their own books, but rather contract with printing and binding firms for this service. Other services as well can be contracted for, such as warehousing and shipping and even sales and promotion, with the consequence that it is possible for very small firms to enter national publishing.

2. Every book must be advertised and sold on its own. This means that a large publisher does not have the overwhelming competitive advantages of greater advertising resources enjoyed by a large manu-

* Reprinted from the September 1963 *Wilson Library Bulletin* by courtesy of The H. W. Wilson Company, New York City.

facturer of automobiles or cosmetics. The advertising budget available for any book depends on the size of the edition rather than the size of the publisher.

3. In contrast to broadcasting — in which it costs the same amount to televise a given program, whether one thousand sets are tuned in or a million — there is a considerable correspondence between the total cost of publishing a book and the number of copies produced. Hence it is possible to publish books for very small audiences indeed. The sale of five thousand copies, or even fewer of a highly specialized book, may suffice to sustain the national publication of a book, even though those sales may take place over many months or even years, while an instant audience of 5 million or more may be necessary to justify a nationwide telecast.

4. In contrast to magazines, newspapers, and broadcasting, books are not supported by their advertising content. Hence, they are published to satisfy the needs or demands of their purchasers rather than to serve as a means of assembling a potential market for a product or group of products.

5. Books are produced in a physical form that permits them to be used by individual readers at times and places of their choice without those readers being assembled as at a theater, or set before a screen or loudspeaker at a predetermined time; to be preserved indefinitely; to be gathered in large collections from which a user can make a choice; and to treat subjects extensively and in detail.

The consequence of these factors is that book publishing is able to be more responsive than any other communications medium to a wide range of diverse demands from audiences large and small. Publishing enterprises can be started with very little capital — where there are three national television networks, there are many hundreds of book publishers selling to a national market. And the smallest of these as well as the largest of them has the opportunity to reach that entire market. Moreover, every publisher can expand or contract his list with great flexibility — he is not confined to twelve or fifty-two issues or required to fill a specified number of broadcast hours.

And the demand to which this complex mechanism responds, which indeed it eagerly seeks out, can be a very small one indeed.

The thousand people who may become interested in the slender volume of a previously unknown poet, the few hundreds concerned with a recondite aspect of Russian research in plasma physics, and the millions who may want an exciting novel are alike served.

Hence the book publishing industry is in many ways an ideal instrument to respond to the extraordinary variety of the metropolis' demands: for complex and specialized information, for a fresh and experimental culture, for mass enjoyments.

But in many ways it is a relatively ineffective instrument. Its ineffectiveness does not arise from its inability to produce books — as we have seen, it can successfully issue them in response to a relatively slight demand — but from its difficulty in distributing them to potential users. In order to understand this problem in general, and in its specific urban context, it will be necessary to examine the distribution structure of the book industry in some detail.

Last year American publishers sold nearly $1,600,000,000 worth of books. Something less than 10 per cent of this total was exported, leaving a domestic book distribution on the order of $1,450,000,000. About $400,000,000 of these were textbooks. Most elementary and high school texts were purchased by local school authorities and provided free of cost to the students. The distribution of these books is hence almost entirely dependent on public authority. In general, the largest urban school systems, hard-pressed for funds as a rule, have made a less adequate provision for textbooks and other teaching materials than the school systems of smaller cities and suburban areas.

The problems of urban textbook distribution have not been entirely quantitative. There are qualitative difficulties as well. The economics of textbook publication makes it highly advantageous to publish for a national market, rather than for a series of geographically or socially differentiated markets. Recently the complaint has been made by a number of large-city educators that most textbooks, aiming at this national market, have addressed themselves to the children of a vaguely defined middle-class, white, suburban or small city population, without providing materials relevant to the experience of the large city, or for that matter, the rural child, or for those reared in poverty or belonging to minority ethnic groups. The preparation and distribution of such specialized materials would, of course, be considerably more expensive than producing for a relatively uniform national market, and though some experiments have been undertaken, no one, including the urban school authorities, has yet been willing to meet the costs involved.

Another approximately $375,000,000 represents domestic sales of encyclopedias. Perhaps 3 per cent to 5 per cent of the sum represents sales to schools and libraries, but the remainder represents sales to individual families by salesmen. Since the price of encyclopedias is necessarily substantial, such sales efforts are directed primarily at middle-class homes.

Of the remainder, about $190,000,000 represents sales of professional works: legal, medical, business, scientific, technical, and university press books. They are published to meet the needs of specialized groups and are nearly all distributed through highly specialized channels. Their ready availability is indispensable to the functioning of the complex activities of any metropolis, but it presents no major problems within the purview of the conference except that of money. The demand for such materials upon college and university libraries and the larger urban libraries usually very considerably exceeds their budgets for purchase.

The real problems of book distribution concern the remaining 850,000,000 to 900,000,000 books published annually, representing sales of about $500,000,000 — of which about one-third are children's books.

The traditional method of distributing these to their appropriate readers is to publicize each new book by advertising it as extensively as funds will permit, by sending copies to a large number of magazines and newspapers in the hope that it will be reviewed, and by achieving as much publicity as possible through whatever means are appropriate. Meanwhile salesmen try to induce bookstores to stock the work so that those who have learned of it in one of these ways may be able to buy it.

Consider the difficulties in this method. There are approximately 20,000 titles published annually in the United States. Perhaps 200,000 backlist titles are in print. Save for the specialized professional books that can be promoted to an identifiable professional group, their potential readers are indistinguishably scattered through the tens of thousands of American communities. Every one of these 20,000 books has to have its own advertising campaign, yet except for a few dozen annual best sellers, their advertising budgets can be only one or two thousand dollars, or even less, with which to hope for a national impact. The largest reviewing service addressed to the public is *The New York Times* Sunday book section. It reviews about one book in eight and reaches less than one home in one hundred. Most books of necessity pass almost entirely unnoticed.

Nor are the channels of actual sale any better. There may be as many as 20,000 establishments in the country that buy books from publishers for resale, but there are probably not more than about 1,500 that seriously attempt to maintain a respectable stock. Few of these have more than two or three thousand out of the 200,000 or more books in print. Most of them are in cities of 50,000 or more or in college towns. An informed guess is that as much as 75 per cent of bookstore sales of hard-cover books takes place in the twenty-five largest metropolitan areas. City folk are hence far better served by bookstores than are residents of smaller communities, but even here the distribution achieved is very limited indeed. Another guess is that the patrons of bookstores in a typical city are fewer than one per cent of its residents. This matches with the fact that probably only about 35,000,000 hard-cover "trade" books, adult and juvenile, were sold to other than libraries last year. If three-quarters of these were indeed sold in the 25 largest metropolitan areas, this is still a sale in those areas of only 27,000,000 books, or less than one-half per capita. For the rest of the country, the situation would be far worse, with sales of about 8 million books to nearly 120 million people, or about one-fifteenth per capita.

Moreover, there were further limitations on the types of books sold through bookstores and the purposes for which they were bought. A high proportion were works of utility: garden books, manuals on bridge, etiquette handbooks, and the like. A very high proportion of the remainder, quite possibly half or more of the total, were bought as gifts. As a general channel for the dissemination of books, therefore, the bookstore in fact served only a very tiny elite within the urban population. This service is of great importance, particularly in the introduction of new writers and new literary trends, in which the bookstore serves a role not unlike that of the legitimate stage in its relation to television and the cinema; but it is not a very meaningful contribution to the general problems of establishing an adequate flow of needed books to the urban population in general.

To escape the limitations of the bookstore as a method of distribution, publishers have developed four other principal channels. One is house-to-house selling, already mentioned in connection with encyclopedias.

In the nineteenth and early twentieth centuries, this was a major means of book distribution for a variety of types of books in the United States, but at the present time the high cost of salesmen prevents its use for anything except relatively expensive sets of books on the sale of which a substantial commission can be earned. Another is selling by direct mail. This, too, imposes high costs, and is practical for only two types of books: specialized works likely to be wanted by members of a particular profession for which there are specialized mailing lists, and relatively expensive works or series for the purchase of which there is usually some concrete motive in addition to the pleasure of reading the work.

The other two methods of distribution, which are applicable to books in general, are both derived from methods of distributing magazines. One is the book club, developed in the late 1920's. This is a method of distributing books by mail to a group of persons who have subscribed in advance and who, unless they request otherwise, receive the books automatically, just as do magazine subscribers. Premiums are offered to new subscribers and the monthly selections are usually offered at less than the retail price. Book dividends are also frequently offered to purchasers.

Recent years have seen the growth of many relatively small and specialized book clubs in such fields as gardening, psychiatry, history, and religion, as well as a number of children's book clubs. Perhaps one hundred different clubs are now in existence, and a good guess would be that about 60,000,000 books a year are distributed through their channels. They embrace a joint membership of several million, and possibly 3 to 5 per cent of the families in America include a book club member. Book clubs hence reach considerably more deeply into the socioeconomic strata than do bookstores in providing material for general reading. They are not, however, nearly so urban-concentrated. Probably cities enroll no more book club members, perhaps even fewer, than their proportionate share of the population. In any event, the book club, requiring some initiative to enroll, the ability to maintain regular payments and the habit of doing so, and a sustained interest in middle-brow books, appeals primarily to the economic and intellectual middle classes. For these it is a most convenient and useful service; but with one exception it does little to penetrate any sector of society not already book-oriented. That exception is the classroom book club, which is not typical of general book club operation. In the classroom book clubs, a group of paperbound books are offered to each participating class each month and a collective order is made up from among the children in the class. There is no individual membership in the club, although the children do individually select the books they wish to buy. The stimulus of the teacher's endorsement and the participation of friends probably does lead children from families not previously interested in books to buy through this channel.

The remaining method of distribution is the sale of inexpensive paperbound books, priced at about the level of magazines, through magazine distributors and wholesalers and through typical magazine outlets, such as newsstands, drugstores, and cigar counters. This method of distribution has grown up since World War II. In part it was made possible by the development of high-speed presses and inexpensive binding techniques and materials. But the principal savings that have made possible the exceptionally low prices of books of this sort have come in distribution rather than in manufacture. Of the price of an ordinary five-dollar novel, over two dollars and seventy-five cents represents costs of distribution: retailers' and wholesalers' discounts, salesmen's salaries and commissions, warehousing and shipping, advertising and promotion. This cost is reduced to twenty-five cents or less in the case of a fifty-cent reprint of the same book, an economy made possible by the mass distribution of 100,000 or more copies through more or less automatic channels.

Distribution of mass-market paperbounds reaches farther into the population than distribution of books through any other commercial channel, not only because the price is lower but also because paperbounds are ubiquitously available. They do not have to be ordered by mail, or subscribed for in book clubs, or sought out in bookstores, but lie across almost everyone's daily path — in kiosks on the street, in the bus or railroad or subway station, in the drugstore, at the cigar counter, even in the schools. Even so, the Gallup poll has estimated that 11 per cent of the population buy 85 per cent of the mass market paperbounds. These figures may be open to some question, but at the broadest estimate even this method of distributing books can hardly be said to bring books to more than one-fifth of the people.

Like book clubs, and in contrast to bookstore sales, the per capita sales of mass market paperbounds seems to be fairly evenly distributed among population centers of various sizes. The largest 25 metropolitan areas, which account for perhaps 75 per cent of bookstore sales, probably account for little more than 40 per cent of paperbound sales. This would amount to about 100,000,000 a year, or a little more than 2 per capita in those areas.

There are also limitations as to the kind of book that can be successfully distributed through mass-market channels for paperbounds. They must be books that can sell 100,000 or more copies without extensive individual advertising, reviews, or promotion — merely upon exposure. This means generally that they must be books already made well known by the success of their hard-cover editions, or books that will have a mass appeal because of their author or subject. Originally it was thought possible to distribute only westerns, mysteries, and light romances in this way. As time has passed, a far wider variety of books, covering indeed almost the whole gamut of literature, has been successfully sold in inexpensive editions. Now there are more than 20,000 paperbound books in print, of which perhaps half are mass-market editions. Nevertheless, limitations remain. Only a national market can usually sustain a mass edition, and the interest in books adequate to provide a sufficiently large market is really to be found only in reasonably literate "middle-brow" circles. Paradoxically, it is far easier to break out of the "middle-brow" pattern of both paperbound and book club publishing in the direction of the "high-brow" than in that of the "low-brow." There are a lot more unskilled laborers than Harvard professors, but the latter buy a lot more books, and it is easier to publish even paperbound books aimed at their interest than at those of the laborer.

This means that the mass-market paperbound is the book industry's best means of reaching the more or less "non-literate" urban audience. They have none of the characteristics of the traditional bookstore or the traditional library or school that might be intimidating to the nonuser of books, they are cheap, and they are physically available. Yet even these "mass-market" books reach only in limited degree those who are not already active book users. This is because that audience simply does not now constitute a large enough market for books aimed at their special interests, and with appropriate vocabulary levels, etc., in Spanish or other languages when necessary, to support either mass distribution or the initial publication of books intended for mass distribution.

What we have been saying is that quantitatively the sale of books in the United States is quite large. Contrary to the general impression, it is in fact perhaps the highest per capita in the world. Commercial distribution is larger than library distribution in large cities. (Statistics, both of book sales and of library circulation, are seriously inadequate. But it is a fair estimate that the annual sale of adult books, other than textbooks and encyclopedias, to individuals in the United States is roughly 6 per capita, measured against the adult population. Library circulation figures are at approximately the same level; but book sales are much larger in large cities than elsewhere, and library circulation per capita is smaller in large cities than in small.) Yet book publication, and more specifically book distribution, is effective only in serving a rather narrow segment of the population very near the top of the socioeconomic-educational pyramid. Book publishing and book distribution, we have pointed out, are very sensitive and flexible in their response to demand — even small, specialized, and minority demands — far more responsive than other media. But it is necessarily to *demand,* rather than to *need,* that the industry responds. The upper strata of this pyramid are aware of the benefits and satisfactions they can obtain from books, and have the sophistication and means to demand the books they want. It is easy to publish for this group, and the books they need exist. In small towns and rural areas, there may not be enough members of this class to support an adequate book distribution, but in the largest cities this is no problem. The highly educated man of means in New York, Chicago, or Boston easily commands an almost infinitely rich informational and cultural resource in books.

A poor and half-educated Negro, Puerto Rican, or recent white immigrant in the same cities may have a far more desperate need for kinds of information available through print. But he is not aware of the need, or that print can serve it, or how and where to get the materials that could help him, nor does he have money to buy them. Without the intervention of some social instrumentality his need is not translated into a demand that can play a role in the economy of book publication and distribution. There is little effective incentive, for example, to publish in Spanish for the Puerto Rican population of New York, or to produce vocational training materials aimed at similar groups, or to produce material for general sale outside the schools that treat subjects of adult interest with simple vocabularies.

In particular, there is little incentive to produce such materials in the massive quantities and to give them the mass distribution that would be required to bring the price very low and physically to reach out to the groups needing to be served.

What are the implications of these facts for the library? I think there are two. One is that the library should be the social instrumentality that can translate the needs of the culturally deprived, of the non–book-using urban groups into a demand, just as the school is, or ought to be, the instrument that translates into a demand their needs for formal educational materials. The library can perceive their needs, has the sophistication to know what kind of printed materials can serve them, and has the means to enter the market place to buy them. If libraries are really interested in buying materials, in some quantities, specially intended to serve the needs of presently non–book-using groups, publishing will rather sensitively and quickly respond to that demand. But if no social instrumentality performs this service — and none will unless the library does — the needs of these groups will remain voiceless and unexpressed, and materials will simply not be published to meet them.

Beyond providing the demand that will stimulate publishing, libraries have the further indispensable function of providing the channel through which books may be brought to presently non–book-using groups. (I should point out that the "non–book-using" group of which I am speaking here embraces not only the seriously disadvantaged groups elsewhere referred to but also a large proportion of the high-school–educated, stably employed, reasonably prosperous elements in the society who for one reason or another cannot easily, or do not, make use of books.) The library is already the most comprehensive book distributing instrument in the country. It has been estimated that, at least in smaller cities, about 25 per cent of the population make some use of the library, as compared with a possible 11 per cent to 20 per cent who buy the paperbounds, 3 per cent to 5 per cent who belong to book clubs, and less than 1 per cent who patronize the bookstore. And it has been pointed out that the necessity for a very large market tends to press book clubs and paperbounds upward rather than downward in the socioeconomic-educational pyramid, since the larger markets are in the middle to upper reaches of that pyramid, in spite of the smaller absolute sizes of the strata at those levels. Hence there is little practical hope, even if more materials appealing to the non–book-using elements in the population were available, that those elements would for a long time to come make up a sufficiently dense market to support mass-marketing distribution methods. It is hence up to the library not only to demand suitable materials for that audience, but also to reach the audience with them.

In spite of splendid efforts undertaken in many cities, the library does not do so very effectively now, as the 25 per cent figure given in the preceding paragraph indicates. In the socioeconomic-educational structure, the library remains primarily a middle-class institution. The reasons are obvious. Public institutions respond to a calculus of demand — as contrasted with a calculus of need — almost as sensitively as does the private economy. The middle-class housewife knows she wants books and what books she wants and knows the library is the place to get them. She will use them if they are in the library and demand them if they are not. The Puerto Rican laborer is not able to assert — nor for that matter is he interested in asserting — such a demand. Because the groups in the society to whose demands the library responds are substantially the same groups as those to whose demands the book industry is also responding, the library intensifies without broadening (except — and they are important exceptions — in children's books and serious nonfiction) the demand for books and spends some part of its resources in filling needs, e.g., for detective stories and light fiction, that could just as easily be filled at the bookstore or newsstand or through the book club. It provides a service that parallels as much as it complements the provision of books through private channels. Meanwhile, both library and industry, for somewhat different but in both cases rather compelling reasons, are likely in the future to have to give even more limited attention to serving the unexpressed needs of the groups of whom we have been speaking.

In the absence of a clear policy determination on the part of the urban authorities who supply libraries with funds, this situation is reasonably certain to get much worse. There are two reasons for this. One is that the library will undoubtedly have to enter over the next decade into an increasingly fierce competition with other social service institutions for state and local funds that will be quite inadequate to meet a whole range of explosive social needs. Relatively, at least, it is more likely to have to curtail the range and quality of its services than to be able to expand them broadly.

The second reason is that urban public libraries are already nearly collapsing under a new wave of demands from groups requiring a highly sophisticated book service, at the opposite end of the spectrum from the needs of the groups we have been discussing. I refer, of course, to the student demand for public library services, which is already the most pressing of the problems of the urban public librarian today. In large part this is now a high-school problem, directly traceable to the poor quality of high-school libraries, their unavailability in evenings and on weekends, and the more demanding level of high-school assignments. But increasingly it will be a college problem. Enrollment in colleges is expected to double in the coming decade. Most of this increase will take place in urban institutions in which the students live at home. For reasons of convenience, and because of the almost certain inadequacy of the library resources of the new or rapidly expanded urban colleges, most of these students will make heavy use of urban public library resources, already used to their uttermost. The consequence is almost certain to be an even further concentration of the acquisitions policy, staff services, and general policy attention of the urban public library upon the needs of a very restricted sector of the intellectual elite. In the absence of a clear policy decision to the contrary, the public library is likely to be incorporated more and more fully into the network of institutions serving research and higher education, to the necessary neglect of those now having limited access to books and limited competence to use them. The probable trend of urban public library service hence will be further to reinforce the book services available through academic libraries and the book trade, rather than to complement those services by vigorous attention to the otherwise unserved. I do not mean to suggest that it is undesirable that the public library play a major role in providing an intellectual elite with complex and sophisticated printed materials. On the contrary, that is an obvious and socially indispensable function for it to perform, and indeed it may well be the most socially efficient use of limited resources. I do mean that unless a radical increase in public library resources can be obtained, and unless pressures on them can be reduced by greatly improved school and college library service, any substantial enlargement in the service to present nonusers will be tragically impossible.

This is, of course, only one aspect of a major problem in what might be called the distribution of intellectual wealth in our society. We have seen the problem rather clearly internationally. It has been fourteen years since President Truman delivered his "Point Four" address setting forth the urgent necessity of measures that would enable the then underdeveloped countries to participate in the advanced technological society of Western Europe and North America. Since that time uncounted dozens of billions of dollars have been spent, principally by the United States but also by the other Western powers and by Russia, to achieve that objective. Yet at the end of fourteen years the gulf between the fully developed and the underdeveloped countries is not smaller but far greater — the gulf in education, in technology, and in standard of living. For every painful yard the underdeveloped countries have progressed, the United States and Western Europe have advanced an easy mile. Nor does there seem to be any practicable way of reversing this process save by a cataclysm that would reduce us all to a primitive equality.

Something similar may be happening within our society. There has always been a stratification of education and trained intellectual competence, more or less correlated with a stratification of income. But in earlier times this was a stratification within a more or less integral society, in which the component parts were reciprocally necessary to each other, in which there were more or less commonly accepted goals, and in which there was a good deal of internal mobility independent of formal education. Today we have to some extent divided internally into two societies: one — at whatever level — participating productively in, and enjoying the fruits of, an extremely high technology; the other largely excluded from that technological order, both as producers and as consumers.

The boundary between these two societies is defined principally by the presence or absence of a realistically effective literacy. The test of useful participation in the technological society is the ability to use efficiently the bodies of print in which the knowledge and procedures of that society are recorded and by which they are conveyed. As those bodies of print and their content become more and more complex, the capacity to use them becomes more difficult to acquire, and the barrier between the two societies becomes more forbidding. At the same time the plight of those excluded becomes more desperate, as employment opportunities narrow and as political comprehension of the actualities of the advanced society dims.

This dichotomy is given a further explosive potential by the facts that today it falls largely along racial lines and that it is most evident in large cities where the extremes of the two societies live side by side in painful contrasts of security, competence, and wealth.

Yet our national policies have the result, if not the object, of further widening this division. Partly impelled by our competition with the Soviet Union, we are devoting many billions of dollars annually to research and development activities that increase the level of complexity of our technology. Billions more go into the development and installations of systems of automation that replace the less skilled. Our principal educational investment in dollars over the next decade will go into the doubling of our facilities for college education, a benefit that can serve only the effectively literate. A doubling of the college-educated class will, of course, further lessen the social utility of the uneducated and enlarge the areas from which they are effectively excluded.

In comparison, the investment of thought and resources in solving the problem of incorporating within the literate culture those now excluded from it is small, though hopefully growing.

The library has always served as one of the means by which unusually gifted and unusually motivated children could escape from the limits of a disadvantaged background and find their way into the literate society. For thousands of individuals in the past it has quite literally opened doors to a new world. Now the developments that have made the nonliterate class obsolete and functionless require not an avenue of escape from that class for exceptional individuals, but rather an instrument for transforming the class itself. This is a new and vastly heavier responsibility for the library, as it is for the schools and the other instruments of society with which it must serve.

The effective dissemination of print through the efforts of the private sector of the economy is confined and will continue to be confined to the middle and upper segments of the socioeconomic-educational pyramid, for only there does a demand exist that is adequate to sustain the machinery of distribution. There necessarily therefore rests on the public sector, on urban schools and on the urban public library, the responsibility for expressing a demand for materials needed by the segments of society not now effectively literate, and for providing a channel of distribution for those materials. This is a responsibility in some degree counter to the pressures on the library to serve the highly literate segments of the society — pressures that will become far more intense with the anticipated more than doubling in urban college enrollment. Yet a failure to discharge this responsibility could, by omission, contribute one more element to an already potentially explosive social situation.

JEROME CUSHMAN

REFLECTIONS OF A LIBRARY ADMINISTRATOR

The American Commitment

The public library movement in the United States fits the general pattern of social and political development of the American people. It is a part of the American commitment. The religious Protestants who came to this land in the seventeenth century followed the Levitical admonition to teach the words of God diligently to their children. Reading was important because its purpose was to teach responsibility — and responsibility in this framework was justification of God's way to man.[1]

In the eighteenth century another force impressed itself upon the American scene. The philosophy of deism presented a personal God who did not interfere directly in the affairs of man. Therefore it became necessary for him to shape his own tomorrows. He stopped waiting for the miracle of deliverance from the everyday problems of his existence, but rather sought ways and means of self-improvement.

The third factor in the American commitment is the vital impulse of the egalitarian concept of Jeffersonian democracy. Man faced the problems of a new society with confidence because he felt that he had a share in the destiny of his country. He acknowledged his debt to European civilization, but in the brashness and fervor of new-found strength said, in the words of Walt Whitman,

> I conn'd old times,
> I sat studying at the feet of great masters,
> Now if eligible O that the great masters might return and study me.[2]

1 R. D. Leigh, *The Public Library in the United States* (New York: Columbia University Press, 1950).

2 Walt Whitman, "Starting from Paumanok," *Leaves of Grass* (New York: Doubleday & Company, Inc., 1940).

The New American became the proud architect of a civilization that took pride in local accomplishments. Schools and libraries were a natural consequence. Great public libraries like those in Boston, Philadelphia, and New York are visible results of interest in local institutions. They are living examples of the American concept, nurtured by the Calvinistic, deistic, and egalitarian philosophies, that education is primarily a matter for local concern.

The Library Faith

There are two hundred years between the development of the concepts of reading for the justification of the ways of God to man and of the importance of reading for its own sake. The latter is called by R. D. Leigh a "library faith," but it did not become a verbalized tenet until the emergence of a corps of professional librarians.[3] The principles of this faith proclaimed that not only are books and reading good in themselves but also the printed word is an important factor in carrying forward the values of western civilization. This leads to the conclusion that the primary task of the public library is educational in nature. It is beyond the scope of this paper to explore more fully what is meant by "educational" in relation to the public library except to say that it must satisfy more than a recreational or reference need in order to discharge its responsibility.

Informed sources are now proclaiming with increasing insistence that education is a national, not a local, problem. Our own library leadership agrees with this concept and is increasing its effort to make the public library more responsive to the general educational needs of the entire community. The interdependence of the schools and the library is well stated on a chart in the September 1961 *Library Trends.* "School libraries fill basic educational needs, college and university libraries are workshops of the academic world and public libraries provide for lifelong learning." An overwhelming majority of librarians subscribed to the accuracy of the library faith as outlined by R. D. Leigh in 1950, and have in effect agreed, in theory at least, to the necessity of a more extensive kind of service.

3 Committee for Economic Development, Research and Policy Committee, *Guiding the Metropolitan Growth.* New York: CED, August 1960.

Students in the Public Library

The urban public library is having a traumatic encounter with today's school population, from junior high through the university. The study by Watts and Simpson, "Students in the Public Library," emphasized that the problem is national. They reported:

> A galloping increase in the school population has come into collision with a new pedagogic emphasis on individualized study, wide and varied reading of non-textbook materials and library research assignments. This collision has precipitated an explosive increase in library use by students. . . . In the past two or three years, concern has changed to alarm and alarm, in some cases, to near panic.[4]

This is a basic concern of the library profession today. The sheer numbers of students coupled with increasing demands have many side effects. Book and periodical collections, the latter almost irreplaceable, are wearing out. Adults, who have no other library facilities except the public library, are being discouraged from its use. Too often every available chair is taken by young people doing their school assignments. School libraries are not able to keep up with the voracious demands of accelerated programs. Many times the large city library is the only one with materials in depth. The public library is fighting a losing battle against preventing damage to encyclopedias, reference works, and expensive sets. The damage sometimes amounts to thousands of dollars per year. Multiple copy needs of students extend every resource of the library. Some institutions are using self-serviced commercial copying machines to relieve the work load of the staff.

The school and the public library, each beset by its own problems, find it difficult to cooperate in buying programs, mutual library hours, class assignments, and teacher-librarian contacts.

Librarians are beginning to feel guilty. In the first place, they want to give good service — and their service capabilities are deteriorating. Second, they want to welcome young people to the library and help them reach their educational potentialities. But their massive institutions, with a total of millions of books, are not keep-

[4] Doris Ryder Watts and Elaine Simpson, "Students in the Public Library," *Wilson Library Bulletin*, November 1962.

ing up with current demands. The "Students in the Public Library" study received replies from almost two thousand libraries in fifty states and eight Canadian provinces. The inescapable conclusion is that no answer has yet been found.[5]

The study "The Metropolitan Area and the Library" speaks about the necessity of removing the barriers between the use of materials for the public, college, and special libraries.[6] The problem of the schools and the libraries was the subject of the inaugural address of James E. Bryan as President of the American Library Association. It is a major concern during his tenure in office, and for the first time in ALA history a conference within a conference — lasting three days — will discuss education and the public library in many of its ramifications.

The Foreign-Born Reader

Every large city has many communities, and the public library should touch them all. The foreign-born population of a city needs special attention because of the importance of individuals making their own contributions to their new country. The Toronto Public Library reported on a study made in 1959 that did more than find out the recreational reading needs of the various ethnic cross-sections in the city.[7] This professional study of population changes in a country not as mobile as the United States points out areas for research by large public libraries which should make their resources more meaningful.

The Nonreader

It seems paradoxical that the librarian who is now having problems because of the influx of people into his buildings should take time to consider the problems of the nonreader. It is logical, though, if one considers a primary function of the public library to be edu-

[5] *Ibid.*

[6] Harold L. Hamill, "The Metropolitan Area and the Library," *Library Quarterly*, January 1961.

[7] Henry C. Campbell, "The Immigrant and the Public Library," *Library Journal*, June 1, 1961.

cation. It is easy to be a nonreader in this country. Television, radio, movies, sports, gardening, volunteer work, and handicraft can absorb one's full time. We need to know more about the nonreader. A drop in reading interest is observed as a child progresses from the grades through junior high and high school. Too many adults consider reading as something to be done in childhood and gratefully put away with other childish aberrations. However, studies of leisure indicate that reading is a meaningful activity for many. Nels Anderson, in *Work and Leisure,* said, "Reading is perhaps the most frequently crossed bridge between our different life interests. For education, the development of personality or for amusement, modern mans turns to reading. More than any other pastime, reading is a lone activity and people differ widely in what they get out of it."[8] We need to find ways of making reading more meaningful for more people. James E. Bryan has said,

> The library's role in education should not be limited to the passive provision of materials but should be so interpreted as to encourage habits of reading, information seeking and reference inquiry that will predispose students to continue their own education informally through their lives.[9]

Cultural Deprivation

The problem of cultural deprivation is demanding the attention of the library in metropolitan areas. This deprivation is tied to the larger issues of education and to some extent social dislocation. More studies need to be made to examine the correlation if any between the use of the library and economic status, ethnic background, race, and educational training. Some librarians are saying that the library needs to re-examine its purchasing policies in order to provide materials which more generally fit the needs of this group. Book collections require examination, lists need to be made, specialized services offered in order to provide an adequate library and educational experience for many who cannot fit into the regular library usage framework.

[8] Nels Anderson, *Work and Leisure* (New York: The Free Press of Glencoe, 1961).

[9] Doris Ryder Watts and Elaine Simpson, *op. cit.*

Adult Education in the Public Library

The adult education movement in the public library has had its ups and downs. Marion E. Hawes said in 1959 that "Libraries are still trying to define or redefine their role in adult education."[10]

There is a leveling off in public library activities in this field since the Fund for Adult Education ceased its activities. Yet many directors of libraries recognize that adult education programming, whether done directly by the library or in conjunction with other community agencies, can make available materials that might otherwise be unused. The important thing about adult education programming in a big library is that it enables the institution to operate across a wide section of community interests. Arranging a program for a political study group, making possible art reproductions for an art association, providing resource bibliographies for people interested in investments, all dramatize the role of the public library as an educational center. The big need has been staff and finances. These two items have prevented all except the largest and best organized libraries from undertaking anything but token adult education programs, but the challenge is still here.

The public library can awaken whole communities to worthwhile projects through carefully planned studies in which both academic and community leadership are involved. The library is a natural material source for information for general community planning. Adult education opportunities for the metropolitan library have an exciting potential. New and more extensive methods should be developed to make it possible for the library to add creative depth to its service.

The Individual Reader

Robert Blakely believes that in the near future such adjectives as "self" and "continuing" education will be dropped and education will mean the life-long process.[11] Every large library has readers who

[10] Marion E. Hawes, "The Role of the Large Public Library in Adult Education," *Library Trends*, July 1959.

[11] Robert Blakely, "Nineteen Eighty (Not Nineteen Eighty-Four)," *Library Trends*, July 1959.

are intellectually curious and who request materials which keep the library staff on its professional toes. Ideas are the stock in trade of such patrons. The very materials they use require that the library give them special attention.

On the other hand, added research is needed to find out more about the good reader. We think that we extend people's horizons, but we are not sure. There is little verifiable evidence of what takes place after the meeting of an individual and a book. The public library will be able to do a better job once it is able to identify more positively the effect of books upon people.

The Professional Staff

Directors of public libraries are more than a little concerned about the future development of their professional staffs. Library school education at this moment is engaged in a soul-searching enterprise. Anxieties are being voiced about the philosophy, content, and end product of library school education. To what extent should library school education provide a training experience for the student? Is the curriculum too humanities-oriented? Does it spend too much time repeating busywork? Will the interest in documentation make for specialist domination in our library schools? Is there any real possibility of the public library, through an in-service training program, taking some of the onerous tasks from the library school? Do the library heads, faced with drastic staff shortages, have the courage to insist upon higher standards of library school applicants?

Recruitment is an ongoing concern of the profession. Its efforts to date are hampered by the tea party approach to the challenge of librarianship. The virtues of the climate and fringe benefits seem to take precedence over the demands of a satisfying professional experience. The realization that a sound financial future appeals as much to an intelligent prospect as the joy of being in a community where there are great cultural advantages is causing administrators to make budget demands in keeping with attracting excellent people. Consideration for a dramatic upswing in the total salary structure for the library professions is a necessary adjunct of any recruitment program.

The Book Collection

There is increasing concern among the directors of large public libraries about the size and condition of the book collection. One correspondent wrote, "Most urban libraries simply do not have enough stock to meet the metropolitan needs now forced upon them."[12] Another reiterated, "The suburban libraries are unable to afford the more technical reference and research materials even though the type of residents of the suburban area dictates that such materials be obtained."[13]

It is difficult for the general public to understand that a large public library with a number of volumes approaching a million is woefully short of materials. Recently a man complained to a librarian in a large city that all of the Spanish language records were in use and he objected to being placed on the waiting list. To clinch his argument he said that while the library evidently did not have enough Spanish language records for public use, it did have thousands of books that were not being used at all. He could have gone on to say, with some accuracy, that the library received many requests for materials which it ought to have but could not afford.

In 1961 public libraries of all sizes did spend around 43 million dollars for books. Yet 57 per cent of public libraries in cities with a population of 100,000 or more, representing 144 out of 255 agencies, had below 100,000 volumes in their collection.[14] A book collection of this size cannot begin to meet the responsibility of a metropolitan library for reference, research, or general reading. Our book collections must expand in order to meet a new emphasis on specialization, research, and changing fields of knowledge.

Interlibrary Cooperation

It seems important to think of some of our great public libraries in terms of scholarly research. Most libraries in metropolitan centers

12 Comments in letters to the author from the directors of the Boston, Brooklyn, Denver, Los Angeles, and Philadelphia public libraries.

13 *Ibid.*

14 *Bowker Annual of Library and Book Trade Information* (New York: R. R. Bowker Company, 1963).

have felt it necessary to make some of their unique holdings available outside their own tax district. It is the continual demands upon their resources without the commensurate additional income to compensate for staff time, replacement of materials, and purchase of new and additional items that are causing the library profession to seek remedies. One area for re-evaluation is in the field of library cooperation. Lending materials between institutions has been a time-honored policy. One librarian put the matter in succinct perspective when he said, "We need to develop more coordination not only between libraries and librarians, but more importantly between academic institutions, industry, commerce and various professional groups."[15] Another said, "Interrelationships of service should exist between all large and small libraries of all types in a metropolitan area."[16] Still another said, "[We need] the development of an adequate formal arrangement between the central core city and the wide surrounding area of both suburbia and exurbia through a useful and viable regional relationship."[17] Actual, not token, cooperation will require special consideration and study in order to make the most effective use of the library's collections.

Documentation

The library profession recognizes the importance of coming to terms with documentation, but many librarians are bewildered by the complicated media. Someone has said that documentation may be defined as librarianship in high gear. We have been a profession in low gear for a long time, and the necessity of using scientific facilities to communicate knowledge across barriers of time, space, and language has come with startling rapidity. Some librarians are claiming that mechanization is the answer and that the future of librarians lies in their warehouse aspect — the more efficient the warehouse, the more efficient the library. Others claim that the library that forgets its commitment to humanism does not fulfill its proper function. Alexandra Mason of the University of Kansas sug-

[15] Comments in letters, *op. cit.* (n. 12).
[16] *Ibid.*
[17] *Ibid.*

gested a logical compromise when she commented, "Surely a humanistic attitude coupled with a technologist's approach can put these together, modify each, and make the resultant product a kind of librarianship which is worthier than either of its predecessors, which is conscious not only of the worth of books and people and is respectful of both, but is concerned with efficient service and is willing to employ new means to this ancient end."[18]

Social Concerns of the Library

Ours is a many-faceted clientele. Its range cuts across community interests and groupings. Business, science and technological, labor, religious, and social needs give to the metropolitan library its variety and its opportunity. Sometimes a library's social concerns appear as large as its educational responsibilities. The words of Wheeler and Goldhor on the subject are to the point.

> A visitor from abroad standing in the midst of a busy American public library is impressed by the sight of so many men, women and children hurrying about to get books and information, or quietly reading and studying in the various departments, or asking reference help at the service desks, or walking out with the books they have borrowed. He observes that most of these individuals get personal help, but no one inquires the name, the status, the politics or religion or the purposes of any one of the library users. . . . Our visitor is looking at a unique manifestation of the democratic process, the freedom of each citizen to read and to think as he may decide for himself, about any subject he chooses.[19]

What effect does the library have on the community? Is this effect measurable? We know that the library is often the focal point of local political, religious, or social dissatisfactions because of the very catholic nature of its materials, but we are often inept in combating these irrationalities. Yet these very irrationalities may drastically reduce a library's effectiveness. Even a large public library can reel from blows caused by frivolous accusations such as "poisoning the minds of our youth, too many dirty novels, blasphemous books, or

[18] *Gamut:* Bulletin of the University of Kansas Staff Association, April 1963.

[19] Joseph L. Wheeler and Herbert Goldhor, *Practical Administration of Public Libraries* (New York: Harper and Row, Publishers, 1962).

not enough material on Americanism." Any look at the future of the urban public library needs to assess its social strengths and weaknesses, its community image, and particularly the question of how to translate the ready-made reservoir of good will accumulated over the years through excellence of service to a position of greater strength.

The Library and Added Support

The poor are not substantial library users, and the rich buy their own books. Those patrons who make the most frequent use of the library are moving to the suburbs, taking with them their patronage of the library. Baltimore and Washington, D.C., are two cities where there have been substantial losses of quality readers to suburbia and exurbia. This, and the loss of many business enterprises to the outer fringe of the city, contribute to the economic crisis facing the metropolitan library today.

The library profession is re-examining its organizational structure in the name of economic and administrative efficiency. There is general agreement that larger patterns of servce are mandatory. One correspondent deplores the degree of duplication of functions and resources between urban and suburban libraries. This duplication, which includes cataloguing, ordering, preparation of bibliographies, reference materials, and publicity efforts, is wasteful of the tax dollar.[20] Another colleague believes that "It is of primary importance to cross community, county and state lines."[21] This broadening of the basis for service necessarily means a new elevation of the traditional support of the library.

The library profession has noted a stiffened resistance on the part of governmental units to request for increased tax dollars. Soaring costs for governmental services contrasts with dwindling sources of revenue. Since the library is a part of the governmental structure, librarians have the comforting feeling that although the boat appears to be leaky, we are all in it together. Therefore the present tendency to search for means to relieve the local unit through a wider tax base is understandable.

20 Comments in letters, *op. cit.*
21 *Ibid.*

The Library and Local Government

The legal and governmental aspects of the public library within the urban framework require a great deal of clarification. In many instances the librarian has no legal status. The library board ranges from being legally responsible for its actions to a yes-man role to the city government or city manager. The powers of the library board are often unclearly defined. There is danger of its succumbing to the prevailing cross currents of the local political climate.

Libraries are hampered by outworn residence requirements for staff and administrative regulations that fit a sanitation department but not necessarily a library. Too many governmental functions have grown without regard for the future. The Committee for Economic Development reported in 1960 that there are 16,000 jurisdictions in fewer than 200 metropolitan areas. "And although our local governments have kept things going they have failed in one crucial area of responsibility: they cannot plan, budget and program ahead for the entire metropolitan region."[22]

The library profession hopes to see changes in the jurisdictional relationships of its responsibilities. The public library is a part of our national educational complex, and efforts need to be made throughout our governmental fabric to make use of strengths whenever they are found. David Clift and Germaine Krettek said, "The nation's library service is clearly in need of bold and imaginative planning and action on an unprecedented scale. Two recurring themes run like a thread . . . a thread that is often bright with promise of opportunity and often somber with the realization of obstacles."[23]

22 Committee for Economic Development, *op. cit.* (n. 3).

23 Frank L. Schick, ed., "The Future of Library Service: Demographic Aspects and Applications," *Library Trends*, October 1961.

PART III

CHANGING STRUCTURE OF CITIES

ROBERT H. SALISBURY

TRENDS IN URBAN POLITICS AND GOVERNMENT: THE EFFECT ON LIBRARY FUNCTIONS

When librarians talked with political scientists in the past, they were fortunate in selecting men who took a modern, or behavioral, approach to political questions. Oliver Garceau's study[1] exemplified an approach to politics which is widely current today. Traditional political scientists rarely mentioned the public library at all, but, if they had, they would have been able to say little that librarians did not already know. Garceau and, more recently, Morton Kroll[2] have discussed the relationship of the public library to the community power structure. Garceau places considerable stress on the tactical issues facing library leaders as they compete in the urban environment for scarce fiscal resources.[3] These enduring problems will be the focus for the remarks which follow.

It is very difficult to establish trends in the development of urban political patterns. Cities are immensely diverse; each community has so much about it that is unique that comparative statements about cities in general have no predictive power. Dahl's study of New Haven suggests some interesting historical patterns; other students, including myself, could generate hypotheses from their knowledge of particular cities. But comparative study to establish commonalities of development and to isolate crucial variables has been largely

1 Oliver Garceau, *The Public Library in the Political Process* (New York: Columbia University Press, 1949).

2 Morton Kroll, *The Public Libraries of the Pacific Northwest.*

3 Garceau observes that public libraries "have scarcely commenced the transition to a public service institution actively sponsored by a broad range of power groups in the community," *op. cit.*, p. 104.

neglected so far. We must rely on a rough summation of single-community studies which, because of differing methodological approaches, are not always comparable. The severity of these limitations is lessened only by the success of an individual scholar's guesswork, and that is a notoriously unreliable basis for analysis.

Recognizing the difficulties, what can be said about trends in urban political/governmental development? A number of demographic points are familiar but bear restating.[4] In the decade just past, core cities in the older metropolitan centers either lost population or gained only a tiny fraction. Their suburban areas continued to grow rapidly, as did core cities in the west and southwest, but the population figures dramatized what many had observed and worried about for some time: core city decay. The loss of population was compounded by the fact that the remaining core city residents were increasingly the very poor, inhabiting slums or public housing and helping to speed the disintegration of the city's physical plant. A shrinking tax base was called on to support increasing demands for public services. The latter partly were demanded by the low-income population of the city and partly were sought by other interests as a means of staving off further decay. All this is familiar, and so are the efforts to cope with problems such as urban renewal, juvenile delinquency programs, and "gray area" education.

The question here is what the socioeconomic changes in the large city meant for the political system. The answer can be found on several levels. At one level the changing population of the city has contributed to a breakdown of the traditional structure of urban politics. Mass emigration from city to suburbs has included a very large proportion of the children of those who *ran* the machine. In many suburban areas today, it is possible to observe the remnants of organization politics, one or two generations removed from the real thing. But the old guard has largely gone from the core city itself. The surviving remnants continue to act out much the same roles as before: "delivered" votes, predicated patronage, and indifference to issues of public policy. But the power is gone. The new immi-

[4] A convenient summary of these data with a discussion of their impact on library service may be found in the issues of *Library Trends,* July–October, 1961, ed. Frank L. Schick.

grants are not effectively mobilized by the organization. It may lack the wherewithal to do the job; or it may lack the spirit to try. In any case, and with few exceptions, organization politics is a feeble shadow of the past.

One consequence of this change is that a large portion of the city's residents are not integrated into the political system. They may vote now and then, but their votes rarely give positive direction to city authority. Without an active party organization there are no institutional channels through which lower- and lower-middle class residents may express their interests. Whether this leads to a more or less active alienation or passive apathy or contented acceptance of benevolent civic progress cannot be answered here. It does mean that the party organizations are now minor elements in the power structure of the city's political system.

Obviously, this was not always the case, and even now the relevance of the parties varies considerably. But the general direction of change seems clear enough. The significance of the change lies not merely in the nonintegration of the citizenry. As the party professionals have lost power, the governmental system has gained it. Fifty years ago the machines struggled to control city authority, which they then manipulated for their own purposes. They did not do fatal damage to most cities, because city authority was far less important to the lives of its residents than now. Far less planning, control, regulation, and economic investment was done by the machine-dominated city than is now the case. (This may be one reason the machine could flourish then and cannot now.) Today urban government has become too important to too many interests to leave it to politicians.

The increased importance of urban government is due in part to the socioeconomic changes which are conveniently summarized in the phrase, "core city decay." Utilities, banks, department stores, and other real estate interests worry about their investments and the metropolitan press articulates the worry. Part of the explanation of increased governmental activity lies in the growth of expertise. We think we know more about such things as crime prevention, public health, delinquency, traffic management, and housing. We persuade taxpayers and voters to underwrite our beliefs and establish broadened governmental programs to cope with problems we now refuse to accept as acts of God. I do not suggest that city government can, in fact, solve the problems of city life; only that there is apparently a broad consensus that it should try.

If the party organization is withering away, who controls this enlarged governmental apparatus? The party was the effective mechanism by which candidates were recruited for public office, and it provided a general posture toward policy questions too. If party is no longer effective and the organization, where it exists at all, must follow rather than lead, who does decide public policy; or, more accurately, who decides who decides?

I would suggest that in city after city we are witnessing a reconvergence of political and economic power. The fragments of city history bearing on the point pretty generally agree that *prior* to the late-nineteenth-century flowering of the machine political office and authority, such as it was, was dominated and even held by the civic elite. The merchants moved in and out of city hall and demonstrated that the notion of a pyramid of power culminating in somebody's bank or board room had both reality *and* reputation. The rise of machine politics, based on the growing low-income population of the industrializing city, had the effect of divorcing political and economic power, giving to each a secure and autonomous base, and forcing each to bargain on the points of their interdependence.

Not only is the political machine withering, the economic and social elite is too. Certainly in many of the older cities (and only a community that is a century or so old could have gone through these cycles) the civic notables have seen their local investments threatened. Some, of course, have been removed from active power by virtue of mergers and amalgamations that make former notables into local branch managers with limited stakes in the local scene. Those who remain, however, have a heightened sense of involvement in and responsibility for their community's economic and social well-being. The remaining notables actively invest time, money, and prestige in urban revitalization.

They do not hold office, of course. Few notables could win elections in communities inhabited predominantly by low-income people. There must be political leadership separate from the notables, but collaborating with them. Candidates for public office today are not dominated by a strong party organization, which frees them to work with the civic elites. I recognize that I have not answered the question: Whence do political leaders now come? The answer is that no effective mechanisms now function to provide political leadership, and almost every city in the nation plays a kind of Russian roulette with itself as a result. The party once served as recruiter and training ground, for better or worse. No mechanism has replaced it.

A third element in the reconvergence, which largely did not exist in earlier times, is "the experts," primarily those technical specialists who preside over the details of operation in each of the major areas of city activity. Possession of expertise is a genuine component of power. As the notables seek to protect their interests, they must ask those with more systematic empirical knowledge what the efficient way to do this is. More and more, the planner, the economist, the social worker, the public health expert, and the like set the agenda for city action and specify the means of accomplishing its tasks.

Leadership — coordination of efforts, communication with the public which must support bond issues, recruiting of personnel, etc. — lies largely in the hands of the elected officials, chiefly the mayor. Part-time personnel and substantial financial resources must come from the civic elites, as must private investment to supplement public undertakings. Substantive planning of programs is the job of the professional. The new collaborative grouping is hardly a power monolith. Power is too broadly shared to be sufficient to accomplish the tasks they set themselves. Urban renewal proposals may be defeated, or, having passed, may fail to attract new business. Blight may outrun building code enforcement. Core city decay may be irreversible. In short, the capacity to achieve power may be inadequate. But what capacity there is lies chiefly in the hands of these three groups, working more or less together.

What is the relevance of these developments for the public library? The library serves the city and is affected by the city. Thus librarians must understand what is happening to its market and to the system that controls it. Most public libraries operate under boards appointed by the city's political leadership; I shall take this pattern to be standard for purposes of this discussion. Some libraries are financed through special library taxes, but it is exceptional when a library does not have to compete with other public agencies for public money. Even where there is a special minimum library tax, bond issue funds must be sought for new construction in competition with other projects. Thus the library is competing for scarce resources, and this is its inescapable political problem.

In any competition for scarce resources, an institution such as the public library must consider what claims it can persuasively make on public funds. In general the limits are set in three ways. One limit is established by the place of the library in the system of community power. Where does the library fit into the urban alliance of economic, political, and technical resources? A second limit is established by the library's public: to what extent are the voters sensitive to library needs? . . . and willing to support them? Note that this is a different and perhaps secondary question. Our thesis is that general public opinion, apart from the power system, counts for much less in securing financial support than our civic mythology suggests. It is not irrelevant, but without support from the power system it is unlikely to be effective. However, without broad public approval, the power system may be unable to secure the necessary electoral approval of tax rates and bond issues.

A third limit is less subject to manipulation. It is the limit of fiscal capacity, which I shall not discuss in any detail. The library's share of public revenue is sufficiently small so that marginal adjustments in library money have only a slight relationship to changes in the city's fiscal picture. It seems fair to say that while a shrinking tax base will, of course, hurt the library, the library's relative share of the public money can potentially be altered, regardless of the over-all size of the pie, with only a small effect on other city services.

Let us turn our attention to the other two points: the library's relationship to the power system, and the library's relationship to its clientele. Since the mayor often appoints the library board, it is structurally possible for the library to be linked to the centers of community power. The question is, whom does he appoint and why? We are not here concerned with the ways in which the board may or may not shape library policy, but rather with their potential role in the political process. Kroll found that a large proportion of the board members in the Northwest were housewives, and that, while they were not themselves powerful, they were reasonably close to the powerful. This may not be an entirely inaccurate statement for the rest of the nation. Board members tend to be close to or acquainted with the civic notables, so that they can establish working contacts if they wish. They are unlikely to have equal access to those segments of the community with numbers but relatively little power: organized labor, Negroes, or political parties.

With the technicians I suspect that a similar relationship exists. That is, the professional librarians, as technicians, can have contacts with other agencies of government, if they try. Contacts with land clearance or housing officials or with welfare agencies are, I would guess, underdeveloped, but not impossible to establish.

Depending on how effectively the lines of communication with those who have power over community resource allocation are developed, the library will fare well or badly in the competition for public money. How would such contacts work? Suppose the library professionals found that existing facilities, especially the branches, were being overrun by adolescents who, especially in the poorer neighborhoods, tended to be rowdy. Possible responses include more rigorous policing, more restricted use, or possibly a flight of facilities to more safely middle-class areas. All or any of these steps might be taken within the library's existing resources and on its own initiative. Alternatively, library personnel might initiate conversations with school, planning, and welfare officials. Some recognition of the general problem of weakened family structure in lower-class neighborhoods might be achieved and physical facilities and programs jointly worked out whereby the library is made an integral part of antidelinquency and antiblight programs. The library might then be able to extend its service in ways that complement the work of other agencies as well as in ways that rank higher in present-day priorities for public money than do books alone. Implicit here is the notion that cooperative alliances with professionals in other public agencies contribute to multipronged attacks upon multifaceted social problems and, in the process, increase the bargaining power of the library in getting appropriations.

These contacts will be crucial when bond issues are necessary for new construction or renovation. The librarian may be able to speak expertly about use patterns and location, but if he cannot also relate those questions to larger issues of city policy, he loses not only effectiveness but also his standing as an expert. If he cannot discuss the contribution of a new branch to neighborhood conservation or the effect of a new central building on downtown redevelopment, his advice must and will be ignored. Libraries do not rank at the top of any city's agenda. It is therefore the task of the librarian to develop the arguments and evidence showing the possible contribution of library service to the functions which outrank it. Again, this is primarily a technical task calling for professional librarians to speak to other professionals.[5]

What of the board in this process? Obviously, whenever board members are able and willing to interpret and relate library needs to other community needs they may contribute to the political strength of the library's case. But insofar as the library's case is a technical case, it is going to be presented by technicians and largely for technicians. The board's function would seem largely to consist of linking the library with other civic needs at another level, that of the civic notables. It is with this group that the board's contacts are likely to be closest; the natural alliance has only to be cultivated. Again, however, library needs do not lead the list of civic demands, and those committed to the library will have to do the cultivation.

One consequence of the convergence of power is that civic institutions are working in closer harmony than they once did. Library boards might be wise to seek out other public institutions in a similar power position and with a similar claim to publc prestige and attention. Cooperatively, they might get more support either from notables or the public than could be achieved separately. In 1961–1962, for example, the St. Louis Public Library collaborated

[5] A striking example of the apparent failure of librarians to integrate their plans with other elements of a city program is reported by Roger B. Francis, "Public Library Site Controversy," *Library Journal,* February 15, 1959. In this case the library board was able to "resist political pressure" and go ahead with its own plans and its own money. In many communities the latter element would not be present, and even in South Bend one wonders how much damage the library's "resolute firmness" may have done to larger redevelopment plans.

with the Zoo and the Art Museum in a campaign to increase the tax levies supporting the three institutions. This campaign involved securing state legislative authorization and city council and voter approval. The last two stages were carried on in conjunction with school tax and bond issues and a dozen other city bond proposals, including one for branch library construction. Several of the issues aroused far more interest and commitment from civic notables than the library proposal alone could have done. There seems little doubt that, to some extent, the latter rode the coattails of the bigger proposals. (The most prominent matter was a proposed new stadium.) This package campaign was headed by a long roster of civic notables and planned by a broad group of professionals in various public agencies. The pattern is fairly well established in St. Louis now and may contain lessons for library officials elsewhere.

Until now we have said very little about the library's clientele and its political uses. One reason for this is my conviction that the library's political prospects are so intertwined with those of other city agencies and programs that any effort to differentiate a library public will, and should, be costly. The library's constituency is a peculiarly mixed one. On the one hand, it has been the preserve of the educated, like art museums and universities, attracting the time, money, and energy of a few devoted spirits and the more passive approval of the WASP. At the same time, it is a refuge of the adolescent, the elderly, and the underprivileged. It attempts to serve the mass and at the same time to nurture the occasional creative individual who escapes here. Librarians, in recent years, have sought to be helpful to any group, in an effort to build as broad a base as possible. At the same time, they have seen their traditional clientele move to the suburbs and have felt the mixed effects of the decline of philanthropy and the rise of taxation as the source of their income.

My personal priorities in a list of library functions would put service to organized groups at the bottom and service to adolescents and senior citizens at the top. Particularly in the older cities, where the middle-class exodus is most marked, the traditional prestige of the library as a civic "good thing" may no longer have much relevance. The startling trends in circulation that show juvenile use increasing so rapidly underscores my earlier point that in today's city the combination of weak family structure and compulsory education leads unprecedented numbers of young people to the library. An effective library program may serve a major welfare function for adolescents and may provide necessary encouragement to the rare creative person among them. My point here is not that a program designed principally for adolescents and senior citizens will bring political rewards. These groups will not, even if they could, vote for increased library service to a much greater extent than their general socioeconomic position would lead them to do. Rather, it will provide an empirical basis for the professional librarian's argument as he presents his case for more public money to other technicians in city agencies. To get the power they need to broaden their resources, librarians must recognize that their function is not simply to get people to read books. Books are the means, of course, but the ends include the prevention of delinquency and blight, and the librarian must be self-conscious about these ends and how he may contribute to them if he is to work more effectively.

A further point may be made: if the library is integrated into the notable-politico-technician establishment, its ability to win public support will equally be integrated. In the St. Louis example, mentioned earlier, votes on the several tax and bond issue questions did not vary more than 3 or 4 per cent, with the library proposals, having received little special notice, following the patterns set by other more prominent issues.

Another political concern of interest to librarians is governmental reorganization. The issue has two main facets: questions of changing the internal structure of city government, and the matter of metropolitan government. An important concern of librarians has been whether the introduction of a city manager form of government may constitute a threat to the autonomy of the professional librarian, and hence a threat to his power.[6] It has been feared that a manager, oriented toward the scrutiny of details of operating procedure, might interpose his judgment concerning, say, personnel selection or book acquisition without having enough appreciation

[6] *See* Carlton B. Joeckel, *The Government of the American Public Library*, pp. 161–169; and James A. Ubel, "Library Board Forms," *Library Trends*, July 1962, pp. 33–34.

of the substantive issues of librarianship. A political mayor would be less likely, it is thought, to interfere at this level. A skillful librarian could ordinarily control his board, with which he is in constant communication. Managers have only rarely been used by large cities, of course, but one suspects that in smaller communities the librarian's fears may often be realized. A manager is trained in the technical areas of budgeting, personnel, and sometimes engineering. He is not professionally trained in areas of city service such as the library, welfare, and education. The manager stands in the same relation to the librarian as any administrator does to his operating personnel. His sympathetic understanding of their needs and problems will never be any better than the professional librarian's ability to communicate with him and command his respect. His perspective is shaped by his training and his job specifications, and neither attaches a high priority to libraries. By the same token, however, it is only the traditional autonomy of the librarian, assured of financial support sufficient to maintain a kind of genteel poverty, that has preserved the institution from more "interference" from administrators in the past. The library, like an industry protected by tariff walls, has had a chance to mature.[7] Now it must compete more directly with other increasing demands on public money and attention. Successful competition will depend less on the structure of government than on the persuasiveness with which the library can be linked functionally with other city needs and programs.

Metropolitan reorganization presents a different set of questions. One side of this involves the level at which service can most efficiently be provided. Earlier discussions tried to arrive at a model allocation of financial responsibility between federal, state and local authorities (e.g., 10 per cent, 25 per cent, and 65 per cent respectively). Similar ideal allocations for servicing could be made. In either case, a metropolitan library agency might fall between the state and local categories. A metropolitan library is clearly a means of extending service to newly developed suburban areas as well as of broadening the tax base for libraries throughout the metropolitan area. Libraries are in the same position as sewers, or police, or other

7 Herbert Goldhor makes this point using the same simile in *A Forum on the "Public Library Inquiry,"* p. 11.

services commonly discussed whenever reorganization on a metropolitan basis is suggested.

There is a complicating factor where libraries are concerned, however. To a significant extent, the increasing suburban population is composed of middle-class people, many of whom are leaving the core city. If the core city library "goes metropolitan," it implies that service emphasis will continue to be given to the relatively well-educated, middle-class homeowners who traditionally have constituted the public library's adult clientele. Direct competition between two rather different types of programs is likely to develop. If, however, separate library organizations serve the city and the suburbs, the core city library may concentrate on its special clientele, while the suburban library may continue more directly in the public library tradition. It seems likely that the separate structural devices would be useful, perhaps essential, as a means of differentiating the attention and programs of librarians. Somewhat greater differentiation would, in turn, improve the bargaining power of the library when it seeks its share of the tax money.

Throughout this paper we have assumed that politics involves the allocation of scarce resources and that, for any particular group or institution, the primary political problem is how to maximize its share of the scarce resources, notably money. There are those whose conception of "the political" is more normative, and who ask not, who gets what? when? and how? but, what is just and good? To this latter question librarians must have answers, but unless they are effectively linked with power their answers remain academic in the most futile sense of the term.[8] The compelling character of power thus has a way of making us all into behavioral political scientists.

8 In stressing the importance of power, I do not intend to disparage the efforts of librarians to win friends in other, less political ways. "Friends of the Library" may often serve a helpful function as links to the larger community and/or as supplementary sources of financial help. *See,* for example, the discussion by Guy B. Garrison, "Friends of the Library: Who Are They?" *Library Journal,* September 15, 1962, pp. 2985–2989. In larger cities, however, "friends" can be of marginal help, at best. Too many other structures of influence exist with greater power and larger stakes for friends to sell the community the case for greater library support.

WILLIAM F. HELLMUTH

TRENDS IN URBAN FISCAL POLICIES: THE EFFECT ON LIBRARY FUNCTIONS

Urban Change

In most of the larger and older metropolitan areas, the central cities are changing in one direction and the suburbs in another. While the populations of metropolitan areas increased by about 23 million during the 1950's to 63 per cent of the population in 1960, populations of the central cities were stable or declined.[1] In contrast to most suburbs, the population of the central city generally is characterized by a lower income level, a lower educational level, a larger percentage of minority groups and of recent migrants to urban centers, a higher percentage of the aged, and more of the socially and culturally underprivileged.[2] Many of the older suburbs and those that are close to the central city have the same problems as the central city.

The location of economic activity in the metropolitan areas is changing.[3] The central city continues to be the center for office and service employment, as shown by the large number of office buildings which have been built in metropolitan areas in recent years. Other types of employment have tended to decline in the older parts and to increase in the newer parts of the metropolitan area. Retail trade is moving from the central city to the new, large, shop-

1 *Statistical Abstract of the United States: 1962* (Washington: U.S. Government Printing Office, 1962), Table 14.

2 *Ibid.*, Table 10.

3 Raymond Vernon, *The Changing Economic Significance of the Central City* (New York: Committee for Economic Development, 1959).

ping centers in the suburbs. Employment in retail trade in the central city of the thirteen largest standard metropolitan areas declined from 78 per cent in 1929 to 63 per cent in 1954. The same shift is apparent in wholesale trade. The central cities' proportion of workers employed by manufacturing concerns declined from 66.5 per cent in 1929 to 57.5 per cent in 1954. In addition to the relative decline, there was an absolute decline in manufacturing employment in seven of the largest metropolitan areas between 1947 and 1954: Boston, Chicago, Detroit, Philadelphia, Pittsburgh, St. Louis, and San Francisco.[4] This movement of manufacturing to the suburbs reflects the fact that these areas are easily accessible by modern highways and are closer to the workers' homes, and that land is available for larger and less expensive plant sites.

Stores, warehouses, factories, and apartments in the downtown areas of central cities are generally inadequate. A number of structures still in good physical condition have become obsolete either because construction styles have changed or because the neighborhoods have changed.

The expenditures of local governments increased about 120 per cent between 1950 and 1961, from $17.0 billion to $37.2 billion. The central city has spent its funds differently from the suburbs. In the city, the increases have been relatively large for welfare, health and hospitals, and public safety. Capital outlays have been used to renovate and replace the existing plant. The largest capital outlay for new facilities has been for highways, freeways, and parking facilities.

In the newer suburbs, there have been large capital outlays for the construction of new schools, streets, police and fire stations, water, storm, and sanitary sewer systems, and the other publicly-provided capital needs in new communities. Increases in current operating expenses have been largest for schools, with expenditures per pupil usually higher than in the city. Capital outlays for schools have been higher since buildings must accommodate large increases in population, where the central city school systems frequently need to accommodate only small increases in population. Total expendi-

4 *Ibid.*, pp. 63–81, based largely on data from manufacturing censuses and business censuses of the U.S. Bureau of the Census.

tures for schools are larger than in the central city and are rising more rapidly.[5]

The major metropolitan areas have income levels distinctly above the national average.[6] Assessed property values and sales of taxable goods per capita in metropolitan areas are above the national average. Thus the economic base from local sources available to support activities of local governments in metropolitan areas appears to be adequate.

There are significant limitations, however, on the ability of these local governments to raise revenue. State laws limit the taxing and borrowing capacities of the local governments: even though a government operates in a relatively rich area, it may not have power to tax the wealth available. Further limitations exist because the many governments in the metropolitan areas compete with one another to keep their own tax rates low and to offer high-quality services in order to attract business and industry.

Local property tax has traditionally been the major revenue source of local governments. This property tax base has been expanding, with new construction and increases in the value of property, but it has not kept up with the increased need for revenues. This has led to a significant increase in the average rates. The property tax still accounts for more than 80 per cent of the taxes collected locally, but sales taxes, local income taxes, and grants from state and federal governments are rising both in amount and in relative importance as sources of revenue.

Fiscal imbalance, an excess of need for expenditures over income, is a pressing problem in the metropolitan areas. Imbalance may exist for a number of different reasons. In a metropolitan area, a

5 Julius Margolis, "Metropolitan Finance Problems," *Public Finances: Needs, Sources, and Utilization* (National Bureau of Economic Research, Princeton, N.J.: Princeton University Press, 1961), pp. 256–258.

6 For example, the median income per family was $6,171 for the State of Ohio, but was above this in ten of the thirteen metropolitan areas in the state, including the seven largest. U.S. Census of Population, 1960, Ohio, *General Social and Economic Characteristics,* Tables 32, 33, 36 (Washington: U.S. Government Printing Office, 1962). The per capita assessed value of taxable property in Cuyahoga County in 1960 was $3,330, against $2,914 for the entire state. (Calculated from Ohio Department of Taxation, *Annual Report–1961,* Tables 37, 43.)

community of modest homes with many children and limited commercial and industrial development may have a comparatively low per capita valuation. Imbalance may also exist because rapid growth has created a great need for public improvements. Capital outlays may rise more rapidly than the tax base, especially when the community is largely residential. Or if a community has chosen to maintain itself as a residential community by keeping out shopping centers and industry, there may be an imbalance. Few communities are rich enough in terms of the average value of homes to be able to support high-quality services without excessive effort.

Some jurisdictions have imbalance due to impractical size. One village in the Cleveland area, which undoubtedly has counterparts in most metropolitan areas in the country, has an area of less than one-half square mile and a total tax of just about $1 million. To maintain a police force with one officer on duty at all times would require a tax rate for this function alone of more than thirty mills.

The decline in the ability of central cities to raise revenue is caused by the decline in the quality of city housing as the middle-income groups migrate to the suburbs, and to the large migration into the central city of persons and families with limited skills and lower educational levels. This may be aggravated by competition between various jurisdictions in a metropolitan area to keep tax rates low.

Various steps have been taken to minimize imbalance. In some states, state aid has been designed to achieve equalization. State aid to metropolitan areas, however, is lower than state aid to nonmetropolitan areas in most states on a per capita basis. In a few areas, such as Toronto, Miami-Dade County, and Nashville, a form of metropolitan government has been established, with some functions performed and financed on a county-district-metropolitan-wide basis.

In some states, local governments have power to levy new or additional taxes; in other states they have developed new sources of revenue. There may be many local income taxes, as in Pennsylvania and Ohio, or additions by municipalities to state sales taxes, such as those in California and Illinois.

In summary, the trends in metropolitan fiscal problems are rising expenditures, increasing pressure on revenue sources to keep up with the needed spending, and imbalances between revenue sources and need in jurisdictions of the same metropolitan area. The economic interdependence of the jurisdictions is increasing, but the increase is not always reflected in political cooperation and consultation.

Effect of Urban Fiscal Policies on Library Functions

Expenditures for libraries have clearly been increasing substantially. Table 1 documents the increase from 1955 to 1961, from $154 million to $368 million. The increase per capita has been from $.93 to $2.01, a faster rate than the over-all increase for government spending. While per capita expenditures of state and local governments have increased about 51 per cent during the 1955–1961 period, expenditures for libraries have increased about 116 per cent.

TABLE 1 DIRECT GENERAL EXPENDITURES OF STATE AND LOCAL GOVERNMENTS FOR LIBRARIES

	Library Expenditures				Total Expenditures All Functions	Per Capita Expenditures	
Year	Total	State	Local	Cities	State and Local Govts.	Libraries	All Functions
	(In millions of dollars)						
1955	154	7	146	128	33,724	$0.93	$204
1956	187*	*	187	135	36,711	1.11	218
1957	199*	*	199	145	40,375	1.17	237
1958	224*	*	224	158	44,851	1.29	259
1959	243*	*	243	173	48,887	1.38	277
1960	278	17	261	185	51,876	1.54	288
1961	368	19	349	210	56,201	2.01	307

* Local libraries only. Direct state expenditures for libraries not included.
Sources: U.S. Bureau of the Census, *Governmental Finances* (annual series); *Summary of City Government Finances in 1961* (Washington, D.C., 1962).

Expenditures have been rising more rapidly for libraries outside the central city than in it. For example, in the Cleveland area library expenditures in the central city increased 130 per cent between 1940 and 1956, while library expenditures outside the central city increased 595 per cent, as indicated in Table 2.

TABLE 2 EXPENDITURES FOR PUBLIC LIBRARIES, CUYAHOGA COUNTY, OHIO: SELECTED YEARS

	Cleveland	County Excluding Cleveland	Total	
1940	*(In thousands of dollars)*			
Current operating expenditures	$1,838	$ 393	$2,231	
Capital outlays	6	5	11	
Total	$1,844	$ 398	$2,242	
Per cent of total expenditures				2.5%
1950				
Current operating expenditures	$3,391	$1,101	$4,492	
Capital outlays	41	345	386	
Total	$3,432	$1,446	$4,878	
Per cent of total expenditures				3.1%
1956				
Current operating expenditures	$4,229	$2,135	$6,364	
Capital outlays	19	639	658	
Total	$4,248	$2,774	$7,022	
Per cent of total expenditures				2.5%

Source: S. Sacks and W. Hellmuth, *Financing Government in a Metropolitan Area: The Cleveland Experience,* Tables III-12, III-13 (New York: The Free Press of Glencoe, 1961).

Library districts in the same metropolitan area spend diverse amounts of money. The range in the Cleveland area is from a low of $1.13 per capita in the area served by the Westlake Public Library to a high of $4.62 per capita in the City of Cleveland. Data for Cuyahoga County indicate that some library districts are giving inadequate service, some are depending on service from other library districts, and some, especially those in the central city, are serving a population much greater than that of their own district.[7]

The data in Table 2 also indicate how the character of expenditures for libraries differs between the central city and the suburbs. In the central city, where the library has generally existed for several decades, library expenditures are almost entirely for current operations, with capital outlays a very small fraction of the budget. The fraction is much larger in the suburbs, where new libraries and branches are being built. In the suburbs of Cleveland, especially in postwar years, capital outlays were about 24 per cent of the total expenditures, while capital outlays for libraries in Cleveland were below 2 per cent in each of the years covered.

TABLE 3 EXPENDITURES OF PUBLIC LIBRARY SYSTEMS SERVING POPULATIONS OVER 50,000: FISCAL YEAR 1960

	Systems Serving Populations 50,000 to 99,999	Systems Serving Populations over 100,000
Number of Libraries	318	255
Population in Library District	21,731,707	80,391,939
Operating Expenditures	$30,979,198	$153,459,898
Capital Expenditures	7,252,080	24,915,205
Total Expenditures	$38,231,278	$178,375,103
Average Expenditure Per Capita	$1.76	$2.23

Source: U.S. Office of Education, *Library Statistics,* OE-15033 (November 1961) and OE-15034 (March 1962).

Table 3 shows that in 1960 library systems serving communities with populations over 100,000 averaged $2.23 per capita of expenditures for public libraries, while systems serving populations of 50,-000 to 100,000 averaged $1.76 per capita.

Another important characteristic of public spending for libraries is "the fiscal insignificance" of these expenditures compared to total

[7] Arlene A. Theuer, *Public Libraries in Cuyahoga County* (Cleveland Metropolitan Services Commission, 1959), Chapter 5.

expenditures.[8] State and local government expenditures of $2.01 per capita for libraries in 1961, as shown in Table 1, were only two-thirds of 1 per cent of the total state and local expenditures per capita. Table 2 shows that Cleveland area libraries accounted for 2.5 per cent to 3.1 per cent of local government expenditures.

The various factors which contribute to growing expenditures — a rising population, especially of the young and the old, rising prices, and prosperity — all contribute to growth in libraries. The population is rising most in the age groups under twenty and over sixty-five. These groups are especially interested in libraries; the young have the formal education and the elderly the leisure time. The rest of the population is also using libraries more.

Prices for personnel services, books, and periodicals, the largest items in library budgets, have risen rapidly. The sharp upward trend apparent in spending data expressed in current dollars becomes a slightly declining trend when expressed in dollars of constant purchasing power. An example from the Cleveland area is shown in Table 4.[9]

TABLE 4 PER CAPITA EXPENDITURES FOR PUBLIC LIBRARIES, IN CURRENT DOLLARS AND CONSTANT DOLLARS, CUYAHOGA COUNTY, OHIO: SELECTED YEARS

	1940	1950	1956
Expenditures per capita, in current dollars	$1.83	$3.23	$4.03
Expenditures per capita, in 1956 dollars	$4.42	$4.11	$4.03

Source: Sacks and Hellmuth, *op. cit.*, Tables III-10, III-11.

Libraries depend for their support on revenues raised by local governments. About 95 per cent of all public funds is provided by local governments; the remaining 5 per cent is obtained from the state. State aid is less likely, however, to go to libraries in metropoli-

[8] Robert D. Leigh, *The Public Library in the United States* (New York: Columbia University Press, 1950), Chapter 8.

[9] This example should be used with caution, as the price deflator used is calculated for all state and local government spending and is not specially designed for libraries.

tan centers than it is to assist local governments in rural areas to provide some library service.

Fees, charges, and fines are another source of library revenues. Fees may be charged for nonresident users, for book reservation, and for certain research services; fines are levied primarily for overdue or damaged books. These sources provide about 5.5 per cent of library revenues, as shown in Table 5. Compared to charges for most other

TABLE 5 CHARGES AS REVENUE SOURCE FOR CITY LIBRARIES COMPARED TO OTHER CITY FUNCTIONS, 1957 VS. 1946

	1957			1946
Function	Revenue from Charges	Expenditure for Function	Ratio of Charges/Exps. (Per cent)	Ratio of Charges/Exps. (Per cent)
	(In millions of dollars)			
Libraries	$ 4.0	$ 72.8	5.5	5.3
Education	39.6	814.7	4.9	2.5
Sanitation	65.7	481.0	13.7	7.6
Hospitals	35.3	351.5	10.1	14.5
Total	$427.5	$5,026.5	8.4%	5.1%

Note: Other functions besides the four listed are included in totals.
Source: The Conference Board, *Use of Service Charges in Local Government,* pp. 28–29 (New York, 1960).

services, library charges have remained relatively constant in proportion to the cost of service. Table 5 shows that they have increased only from 5.3 per cent in 1946 to 5.5 per cent in 1957.

Gifts for current use and for endowment are still another source of revenue, but are relatively small. At times this limited support may provide as much as the site for a library or a wing of a building.

Implication of Trends for Financing Metropolitan Libraries

The metropolitan area offers an excellent opportunity for libraries to cooperate in interlibrary loans, special research collections, exhibits, the operation of binderies, photocopy services, lectures, maps, and other important services. Changes in the population of the central city have made the main library both the major library in the metropolitan area and a research center for business and professional use. Its importance as a research center will increase as research activities grow in the central city.

Branch libraries are frequently located in neighborhoods which have changed their character, as the traditional high-frequency users of the library from the middle income families have moved to the suburbs. Branch libraries in the now lower-income residential neighborhoods are valuable because the residents have relatively few books in their homes and their access to books is primarily through schools and libraries. The libraries must now provide programs contributing to literacy, improved educational levels, higher horizons and enrichments, and recreation. Librarians must work effectively with other governmental and private agencies in the metropolitan areas, especially with the public schools, recreation, and social agencies, to do this. Libraries also may have opportunities to relocate or improve their services in areas experiencing urban renewal and housing developments. The location of new branches should be decided on a metropolitan-wide basis. New areas might be served by bookmobiles or other transient library facilities until a permanent library can be started efficiently.

In the rapidly growing suburbs, instead of branch libraries with no users there are now users but inadequate libraries. The variety and quality of library services are very uneven. In the older suburbs, the libraries frequently are strong and well developed, with programs to meet community needs and interests. In the newer areas, the problem is to prevent the libraries from lagging too far behind the population. In these areas, services such as new schools and streets compete with libraries at budget-making time, and may carry a greater sense of urgency. The libraries need someone to speak up and get 2 per cent of the budget for them. The high interest of the suburbanites in children and schools strengthens the libraries' case for a place in the budget. Some suburbs may find it most efficient to contract for library services from the county or from an adjacent municipality with a well-developed library.

County governments, or other governments serving all or a large part of the metropolitan area, can provide library services more efficiently than can the numerous municipalities in the county. It is desirable that any state aid program encourage local communities to coordinate and cooperate — and perhaps even to consolidate — to provide the best services at minimum cost. Any level of government that provides assistance to libraries in metropolitan areas should be sure that library services are at a reasonable minimum throughout the metropolitan area.

The financial incentives should be geared to help those jurisdictions least able, in terms of the local tax base, to provide services for themselves. New arrangements for providing revenue on a metropolitan-wide basis are under examination in many of the 212 metropolitan areas. A metropolitan-wide property tax would be a more equitable way of financing metropolitan-wide library services than separate property taxes collected by various library districts. A metropolitan-wide sales tax, income tax, or value-added tax are other alternatives which would produce substantial revenue to relieve the overworked and inequitable property tax.

From the point of view of libraries, it would be desirable to have earmarked taxes on which the libraries would have sole or first claim. From the point of view of good budgeting, however, segregating and earmarking revenues for particular purposes does not lead to greatest efficiency. The need met by the earmarked tax may change, and the particular function financed by the earmarked tax may be carried out either on a gold-plated basis or on a starvation basis if the need for the service does not change at the same rate as the revenue from the earmarked tax.

Libraries receiving financial support on a metropolitan-wide basis should be expected to make available their facilities and services to all inhabitants of the metropolitan area. An efficient development of library resources in the metropolitan area would require one or more large library systems with a wide range of services. Consolidation of library districts would eliminate competition for funds, duplication of specialized services, and the many technical service operations. One library board could plan the location of facilities and the provision and expansion of services for the entire metropolitan area. The public library system could coordinate efforts effectively with private university libraries, private research centers, and public educational institutions.

The community orientation of the separate libraries could be continued by encouraging contributions from municipalities, boards of education, and private groups and individuals for the benefit of particular branch or area libraries.

In summary, public libraries in metropolitan areas face rising expenditures, expanding pressures for more revenues, diversity of service levels between different jurisdictions within the metropolitan area, and imbalance between needs and resources. Libraries have an advantage in that their budgets are relatively small and are not a decisive factor in major fiscal changes, such as a sharp increase in the property tax rate. Dedicated and effective support from library users can usually justify the library budget, although generally at a level below that recommended by the American Library Association. On the other hand, public libraries do not have the emotional appeal, broad public contact, and visibility of the public schools. Thus large expenditure increases, especially if they must be voted separately, may be difficult to achieve.

The library system in the central city will continue to provide the most important library service to the entire metropolitan area. Reliance on this library system may well increase, regardless of any decline in the population of the central city.

Any changes toward metropolitan-area government will probably include libraries. Some special districts or county governments already provide library service over areas broader than those served by single municipalities in metropolitan areas.

Urban libraries should expect to fare well provided they offer efficient and high-quality service and cooperate on a broad basis with other public and private libraries in the metropolitan area.

PART IV

OLD PROBLEMS, NEW THINKING

EMERSON GREENAWAY

THE LIBRARY FACES THE FUTURE

During the 150 years since the founding of the first public library in this country, the pattern of library service has remained much the same and development has been very slow. Probably the greatest deterrent to rapid growth is the fact that library service is dependent on permissive legislation, whereas education, at least at the elementary and secondary levels, is mandatory. The picture is complex; a solution will not easily be had.

The metropolitan public library of tomorrow faces tremendous obstacles and problems. Our cities are changing both as to population and as to the composition and characteristics of the residents. There is a flight of businesses and of people from the city and a development of new and smaller businesses in the suburbs. There is a multifaceted change in the living patterns of these people. Communication is vastly different than it was when public libraries were first established. New inventions mean things can be done differently in tomorrow's world. The educational process is nothing like it was in the past. There are changes coming in our governmental structure which will establish new patterns of operation and forge realignment in the present tax structure. All these and many more factors will affect the metropolitan library's growth, development, and role in the future.

There is no one substitute for the public library. It serves all people from the time they can first look at a picture book until the senior citizen reads his last book — and they are living and reading at a more advanced age today than when public libraries were first established. These demands call for a wide service program, vast collections of library resources, a tremendous organization, and numerous outlets or agencies.

The city has lost residents in the higher educational-cultural income bracket. Their places have been taken by persons with minimal resources. It is not unusual to find a higher reading per capita figure in the suburban communities, but the reference use of the metropolitan library is usually greater. A study of persons served by branch libraries in almost any large American city will show the same pattern of change, which affects the work of the branch not only as to collections in relation to age levels, but also as to services given. In fact, many branches have been closed and the collections redistributed or moved. And now, in many of our eastern cities, the cycle is complete, for with urban redevelopment, high rise apartments, and the use of air conditioning, people who moved out into the suburban areas a generation or two ago are now moving back; but whether they will again become a factor in the political and governmental life of the metropolitan city remains to be seen. It should be noted that while the new suburban resident eventually got what he wanted in the way of new streets, schools, parks and recreational areas, and a small town library, he did not have available to him the major resources of a large metropolitan library. For the most part it was the high school student in the family who suffered, for the breadwinner, working in the city, usually had access to the central library, its collections, and its services.

Conversely, the businesses which located their new plants on the periphery of the city had no major collections to rely upon and either had to develop their own special libraries or had to make arrangements with a college or university library to use the materials they required.

All these developments have naturally resulted in a change in the living patterns of the residents, as farmlands and country estates became subdivided, bringing hordes of people from the cities. Public libraries in the towns and villages were taxed to capacity, but largely for recreational reading — for the overwhelming change in the use of the public library as a source for educational materials had not yet developed. Many of the suburbanites were still dependent upon the city for most of their goods and services. Then came the suburban shopping centers, the construction of high speed arterial highways and greater mobility, radically changing their patterns of living. In spite of these new conditions the public libraries in these small centers of population could not amass the resources to be found in the major metropolitan library. Students as well as adults were totally dependent on them as a resource center.

In the 1950's there occurred a new phenomenon in regard to the use of libraries by students. Many public librarians reacted in horror to the influx of secondary school students who were assigned "research" problems and who were directed to make a new kind of use of public library materials. Assignments were often made by teachers who had not verified whether material was available in branch libraries, thus forcing the high school student to use the distant central library facilities. Sometimes assignments were made when no material was available anywhere. Today many public libraries report that up to 75 per cent of their clientele is students. Something has to give — the status quo, the adult, the student, or the librarian. The suburban and day college student must have access to major library resources not to be found in the town or branch library.

The demand for a new department and cabinet officer for urban affairs and the various state legislative committees dealing with metropolitan problems indicate that within the foreseeable future new solutions will be found to old problems. Libraries are in an advantageous situation, having a detached place in the minds of the public and the government. Because they are thought of as educational and cultural institutions by the public and not attached to local politics, they may stand a fair chance of being one of the metropolitan services that all would support. Solutions to problems involving taxation, capital improvements, service programs, and the preservation of local pride can, I believe, be worked out equitably and satisfactorily.

In spite of the progress made by librarians in many areas, we are so compartmentalized in our thinking of problems by types of libraries that we forget library service as a whole and for the total population. The years of struggle to develop and improve the school library, the college library, the special library, and the public library have led to parochial programs and narrow points of view. While each type of library has achieved some success, no institution has nearly solved all the problems or acquired enough materials and resources to be completely independent from any other.

The public library receives the overflow of students from the school or college library, and the adult tends to be squeezed out of the library. We might ask ourselves to define fully the role of our specific institution (and some have already done this) and then examine our resources to see if we can match deeds with words. This would be helpful, but I think we should be bolder, and ask ourselves: What is the best library service we can give to the total population?

A national commission, federally constituted and financed, will be required to study and make recommendations for future objectives and services. A commission composed of leaders in education, government, and the political and social sciences and backed by a strong research staff could make influential recommendations for total library service. A fraction of the money now used for library services would be well spent on a broad research program.

One possibility would be a recommendation to establish a Department of Libraries at all three levels of government — federal, state, and local. Such an arm of government would be responsible for all library services no matter where given.

The study would be long and expensive, and the conclusions would undoubtedly require changes in our thinking, financing, organization, and service programs. This would not be easy. But already there are indications of great changes to come, in New York, Pennsylvania, Massachusetts, and elsewhere. The idea of systems of libraries, long discussed by librarians, is coming into being in the public library field. But we must examine any plan in terms of total library service. Illinois is seriously studying the problem of total library service, and other states and regions will follow.

All this is of the greatest importance to the metropolitan library, which serves also as a school, college, special, public, and regional library. What is its future? Should it redefine — or define — its purpose? What should be its relationship to other kinds of libraries? Should it be operated by the state rather than by the city? If adjacent to other states, should they also contribute to its support? How can local interests and responsibilities be preserved, if they should be? How can private and tax-supported libraries work together? These and many other questions must be raised and answered.

In 1956 Philadelphia adopted a plan of regional library service within the city. Three types of library service were to be developed: first, basic service through forty to forty-five neighborhood branch libraries with collections of usually not more than 40,000 volumes; second, service through five regional libraries with collections of up to 200,000 volumes, giving emphasis to reference, nonfiction, and periodicals; and third, at the apex, the central library with its specialized holdings. The first regional library will open in October of this year, the second is provided for in the capital program, and the others will come later. Once the program is completed, Philadelphia will have as complete public library coverage as we can plan for — but will still have many problems. We are in the process of establishing a Library Council of the Philadelphia Area, which we hope will enable us to solve many problems on a cooperative basis.

The Martin study on Pennsylvania public libraries, released in 1958, resulted in the passage by the state legislature of the Library Code in 1961, which was the most important library event in the state since the founding of the Library Company of Philadelphia by Benjamin Franklin in 1731. The state now has complete library coverage, although it will be at least a decade before there is great strength in many presently underdeveloped areas. The plan calls for a voluntary system of libraries to provide three levels of service, in order to give full geographic as well as resource coverage. At the base of this system is the local library; all residents of the state will be within a half hour's drive of a public library. Local communities may either establish a library or contract with a larger library providing they establish within a stated period of time a per capita support of two dollars or a half mill tax on the real market value of the community, whichever is less. All control and administration of the library is in the hands of the local board of trustees. The state will provide up to 25 cents per person residing in the library's service area.

All local libraries are included in one of thirty library districts, with a district center library within one hour's driving time of all its residents. The district center receives up to 25 cents additional support for each resident of the district living outside the center's local taxing area. The local libraries may request advice and assistance on book selection, library management, or service programs. Free interlibrary loan service is available and reference service, either by telephone or in the district center, is available to all residents.

The capstone to this program consists of four regional resource libraries — the Carnegie Library in Pittsburgh, the State University at University Park, the State Library in Harrisburg, and the Free Library of Philadelphia — which can be reached within a day's time, for research and study purposes. Eventually the state will allocate $100,000 annually to each of these libraries to improve the collections and to make available to the entire state resources and research facilities that no library could possibly supply using local funds. These resource libraries, giving strong fiscal support to the Union Library Catalogue of the Philadelphia Metropolitan Area, will be able to supply the bulk of materials needed in Pennsylvania, securing interlibrary loans from outside the state only for the rare, older, less used or exceedingly expensive or specialized materials.

Under this program, Pennsylvania's library resources and services will be brought to new levels of excellence. But it is important also to raise the level of library service in both the academic and the special library areas. As with public libraries, very few academic libraries meet established standards now; when the schools attain the enrollments expected in the next decade or two, something will have to be done about their collections, services, and buildings. When the academic libraries don't have enough books, when they don't have a full service program, and when they aren't open enough hours, the students are going to spill over into the public library. The public library then becomes an educational institution in a limited sense. Its primary role of service to adults and the cultural development of children is negated.

If we can solve the church-state problem and satisfactorily finance school and academic libraries, perhaps we can then realign library services and create a new library service program. If in a metropolitan area we could have libraries for children's recreational reading and to stretch their growing minds, leaving to the schools the reference work and the supplying of curriculum-related materials; if we could have student centers to take care of high school and college undergraduate materials and services; and if we could have adult collections for the graduate student, the faculty, and the postschool adult; could we not provide better services for all?

Epilogue

Since this paper was prepared in 1963, significant changes have taken place at the national level in regard to libraries and the services they give. That was the year the late President Kennedy introduced an omnibus education bill. This bill, with its general provisions for education, would also have affected all types of libraries and would have provided funds for library resources, construction of library buildings and the training of librarians. The bill, however, was broken into several parts; some sections remained in committee and some were enacted into law.

The first section to be passed was the Higher Education Facilities Act, which provided grants and loans for the construction of undergraduate and graduate facilities, including libraries. Although funds for additional library resources were not included in the final bill, the passage of this bill was highly important to academic libraries.

The next section of the omnibus bill to be legislated was the Library Services and Construction Act of 1964, which contained provisions for public libraries. The old Library Services Act which provided rural library services only was superseded. The new act removed the population limitations and permitted both rural and urban public libraries, regardless of size of community served, to participate under the provisions of the new act. The scope of the act was expanded whereby a new construction title was added and the District of Columbia was brought within the coverage of the act. The raising of the budgeted money from $7,500,000 to $55,000,000 was a giant step. This act expires June 30, 1966, and must be renewed and refinanced at a higher level by that time. Larger appropriations are necessary to make possible adequate financing of libraries at the local level.

Direct legislation for school libraries was blocked by the church-state impasse. However, significant gains were made through the National Defense Education Act and in its extension, which is to run to June 30, 1968. Libraries and librarians are recognized throughout the law, provision being made for the training of school librarians as well as for the purchase of materials.

The Economic Opportunity Act of 1964 has great implications for public libraries by making it possible for them to provide services to those of limited economic means. Libraries working with other community agencies could develop new techniques, using new materials to make readers out of nonreaders.

Libraries have been mentioned increasingly in recent years by our Presidents. President Kennedy, in submitting his recommendations for the National Education Improvement Act of 1963, included references to the importance of libraries. In his Special Education Message, he stated:

> Education is the keystone in the arch of freedom and progress. . . . For the individual, the doors to the school house, to the library and to the college lead to the richest treasures of our open society . . . .

President Johnson, in his special Message on Education, January 12, 1965, over and over again included provisions for libraries as a necessary part to carry out his proposals "to put the American dream to work in meeting the new demands for a new day." Although not yet enacted, there are provisions in the bills introduced to carry out his recommendations, to improve school, academic, and to a considerable extent, public, libraries. This would be done by improving resources, providing supplementary educational centers and services, regional education laboratories, and by strengthening state educational agencies. Aid would be given to preschool programs, elementary and secondary schools, and to colleges and universities. Of special interest is the recognition of the training of librarians and the need for research. Educators and librarians alike will follow the debates on both the Elementary and Secondary Education Act of 1965 and its companion bill The Higher Education Act of 1965. The passage of these two bills is of the highest importance to our broad educational program.

The problem facing librarians now becomes one of making the most effective and efficient use of the federal funds as they are appropriated and in keeping a balance between federal, state, and local monies. We are now being given the means to do a job long dreamed of.

RALPH W. CONANT AND RALPH BLASINGAME, JR.

SOME RESEARCH QUESTIONS

The purpose of this paper is to suggest areas of research that are likely to provide useful guidelines for public librarians in their search for appropriate ways to adapt to social, political, and economic change in cities of the United States. The topics are by no means exhaustive, but they do include areas where significant gaps in relevant knowledge occur.

Libraries, like many other subsidized public services, lack built-in sensitivity to shifts in demand for services. This defect is no problem from the standpoint of institutional survival unless the shifts impair the ability of libraries to justify services. Banfield asserts that many library services are already obsolete or are the business of some other public or private agency. If he is right, libraries that fail to reevaluate objectives in terms of current demands may find their support gradually dwindling relative to other services.

The problem of the urban public library and the problem of every urban institution whose constituency is locally based is how to sense factors of change that affect demand for the product and service offered. Successful private enterprise typically places a high value on market research, program evaluation, and organizational self-criticism. These are not activities meant only for superprofit corporations. Competent market research spots shifts in established markets and senses potential new markets. Competent program evaluation correctly assesses fit between current programs and market demand as well as organizational capacity to adapt to new demands.

Public enterprises are typically not judged by profit-and-loss statements, and because they lack so demanding an incentive they do not always feel a pressing need to justify activities in terms of response to market. Thus market research and program evaluation are not given high priority. Traditional justifications are used year after year to support budget recommendations. Public libraries, like so many other public institutions, vary in their ability and incentive to maintain sensitivity to demand for their services. Some library administrators know their markets and know how to adjust services to changing demands. Most do not.

Nevertheless, leaders in the public library world have for many years been keenly aware of the need to develop a set of research tools with which administrators and library leaders can shape new policies for local, metropolitan, and state library services. Past efforts at establishing major library research have apparently failed to gain a favored place among the permanent commitments of the profession, maybe because the library intelligentsia have traditionally placed a greater emphasis on administrative skill than on scholarship.

A way out of the dilemma in the past has been to call on the social scientists for serious research on the library. Outstanding examples are Berelson's *The Library Public* (1949), Garceau's *The Public Library in the Political Process* (1949), and Alice Bryan's *The Public Librarian* from the Public Library Inquiry.

One of the purposes of the Endicott House Conference was to revive interest among social scientists in the problems of the urban library. The 1964–1965 Rutgers seminar on problems of libraries in metropolitan areas was aimed at persuading social scientists to help with the task of developing a set of research proposals on library services and functions and to persuade librarians to accept these proposals as high priority aims.

The Library's Market

One major area of research for libraries is investigation of consumer trends and tastes. Who are the present customers of the library? Who were customers a few years ago and dropped away? Why? Who are likely library users five or ten years hence? How are social and economic trends in urban library market areas likely to affect library use in these areas? Will present customers of the urban public library stay put? Will others replace those who do not stay? What new services and facilities should be developed to meet potential markets among current users?

Some of the papers in this volume implicitly or explicitly suggest that public libraries should reshape services for special appeal to the urban poor. Are there in fact untapped markets among the urban poor for services and facilities which librarians are peculiarly competent to develop? Librarians know that the poor do not use libraries to any great extent. They know that for people to use library materials, these must be both accessible and relevant. But they do not know enough about how to shape library programs so as to solve either the accessibility or the relevance problems for this group of potential clients. They must learn how to bring such people and books together, and what sorts of materials would be relevant for them.

These problems cannot be solved by asking limited questions. Both "accessibility" and "relevance" depend on what people find interesting and why, where they feel comfortable going, with whom they like to interact and in what ways — in sum, with their entire style of life. Research designed to make libraries accessible and useful to the poor should approach communication in its whole social and cultural context, in the same way that Richard Hoggart's inquiry into *The Uses of Literacy* in England came to develop a classic analysis of British working class culture as a whole.

Librarians could benefit by research into the culture of urban poverty which would focus on the uses which the printed word now has for the poor — whether of entertainment, information, or self-definition — and of the other sources of ideas, information, and entertainment with which reading competes or to which it relates.

Such research should also focus on some hypotheses as to the sorts of reading experience which may contribute to the learning of skills and redefinition of the self which might help people move out of the poverty level.

Some more general questions on library users are these: What are the social and economic characteristics of urban library customers? What are the similarities and differences, if any, between users of the central city library and those who use branches and suburban libraries? How do the salient characteristics of users compare with those of the general population? What are the implications of the findings for library services?

Little has been done to investigate the growing disparity between the public library of town and suburb and the public library of the metropolis. In contrast to the suburban library, the big city library takes on aspects of a research institution, supplying to the business and scientific community and to the advanced students and staff of the higher schools and universities specialized materials which cannot be acquired by the suburban and village libraries. The increased demand made on the city library, especially in these days of cooperative development, when it is often the hub of a state-wide network of libraries, makes its role increasingly unique.

What are the long-range changes in individual libraries in demands for materials and services and in characteristics of clientele? Do such factors as education, social and economic status, and occupation relate to specific demands upon the library as revealed by choice of books or reference questions asked?

Functions of Libraries

No one knows exactly how librarians spend their workday time nor precisely how much library money is spent on specific library functions. Likewise there is no reliable knowledge on who benefits from specific library services. Intensive time-budget studies would reveal in detail how library staff members spend typical workdays and thus how funds allocated to staff services are spent. These data, added to other specific library costs, could be compared to a detailed analysis of customer use. The objective would be to determine who benefits from library services and at what cost. One might discover that housewives who read best-seller fiction place a weighty cost burden on the public library as compared to the "serious reader" Banfield favors, or that libraries already serve the public purpose for which Banfield argues. In any case such research would produce valuable tools for the library administrator and extremely useful data for officials who shape library policy.

Any investigation of users and uses of libraries should also include a close look at the competing suppliers of the intellectual goods the library offers — paperbacks, book clubs, television, newspapers, etc. Philip Ennis' work is suggestive of this line of research.

The Political Environment of the Public Library

Oliver Garceau wrote in 1949 in *The Public Library in the Political Process* as follows: "In political campaigns carried on by the library, the main armament is still supplied by eighteenth century rationalists." And he observes: "[A] particular interest, committed to a traditional body of thought, must exercise sustained political skill in reintegrating its own social myths in the total pattern of ideas."

In effect Garceau says to the librarian: "You have your tradition and you are stuck with it, like it or not. But you must not fail to restate your rationale in the idiom of the times." We have urged librarians to consider investigations that might lead to reshaping library policy to adapt programs to the changing social needs of the city. Here we urge librarians to consider questions that might lead to profitable adaptations to the shifting political environment in which the urban library finds itself. Garceau began the work. We restate the central questions: Who makes the decisions on the level of financial support for the public library? To what extent do these decisions reflect community opinion? What is the role of the library administrator in determining the main objectives and basic policy of the library — of the library trustees? To what extent are library policy makers represented in the "power structure" of the community? What difference does it make either way?

The Objectives of the Library

Even if the traditional rationale of the public library is to be taken as intractable by library professionals, an outsider's analysis of institutional theory and practice could be of immense value to library leaders who wish to deal realistically with the capacity of urban public libraries to retain an influential place in cities.

What are the stated objectives of libraries and the library profession? How do the stated objectives affect the ability of libraries to adapt to urban change? How do stated objectives compare with actual objectives as revealed in time-budget and unit expenditure studies? If stated and actual objectives differ, what functions do each serve? Do library users impute objectives to libraries of which librarians are unaware? What influence do imputed objectives have on library service?

The Image of the Library

The library establishment is in many respects an in-group professional system capable of organizational reactions which may selectively encourage or discourage library use. The library institutions may have characteristics which aid innovation or retard innovation, which affect its ability to obtain financial support and which attract or repel able people. What attitudes, organizational characteristics, traditional modes of operation constitute real or perceived obstacles to use by the urban poor, by youth, the aged, and other specific categories of nonusers? How important have these factors been in determining the present categories of regular users? What types of services are typical library staff members prepared to supply because of personal background, attitudes, or temperament?

The Education of Librarians

Schools of library service, like law schools and medical schools, should recruit and train candidates, provide intellectual leadership, sponsor innovative research, invent new administrative procedures, and in a variety of ways re-enforce professional values and traditions. Their strategic position in the profession should make them extremely influential in the shaping of new ideas and in the reshaping of old ones. Indeed the library schools may importantly determine whether new ideas ever come into currency at all and whether old ones ever get reshaped.

An objective analysis of curricula, research programs, and modes of faculty and student selection would reveal a great deal about the real aims and aspirations of the library profession and much about its adaptive potential.

What are library students expected to learn before, during, and after library school? What are the principal objectives of the formal training? How do the training objectives square with what is expected of the career librarian? What kinds of recruits do the training and career expectations attract? Are library educators satisfied with the caliber of students their programs attract? Are library administrators satisfied with library school products? Do library school research and teaching programs encourage intellectual and technical innovation? To what extent is the emphasis of teaching and research on perpetuating tradition? What are the main standards governing the selection of library school faculty members? What are the main consequences of the faculty selection policies? for research and curricula? for prestige of the library school in the profession? for attracting able students? for creative leadership of library institutions?

There are other possible areas of research on libraries. For example, we are tempted to suggest a variety of administrative and management studies which might improve current services, but we have purposely avoided such questions in favor of categories of research that in our judgment would contribute to an understanding of the fundamental conditions of the urban library and the human and physical environment of which it is a part. Thus we seek to encourage the library administrator and the library scholar to rethink the concepts by which his profession and institutions are bound.

PART V

THE CRITIC SPEAKS

JOHN E. BURCHARD

THE CRITIC SPEAKS

These discussions have often reminded me of Haydn's Farewell Symphony, with an important difference: there the performers played in concert until they tiptoed out.

Until Mr. Lacy's excellent and thoughtful paper, I felt more than a vague uneasiness about this set of meetings. But he has put things, I think, in their proper perspective, and spared me the necessity of saying a number of things which I should have said in a less good-tempered way.

Perhaps we did spend too much tender-skin time trying to establish or debate a well-known historical fact, that some important creative people have come from the slums. Not all creative people have come from the slums, however. It is a distortion of the evidence to suggest that all or most of the cultural drive has come from the urban lower depths — or the heartland, or Oxford, Mississippi, or any other place you want to mention — because this will lead one to define great writers by their origins, which is a rather bad way to do it. Anyway, all this was largely irrelevant to our problem. It is also true, and I think not very relevant, that the language of the lower classes has always served to modify the standard language; so has the language of other groups, for example, the astronauts of today with their "A-OK" and "everything go," and the engineers, with such repulsive words as "feedback." This is inevitable, even desirable up to a point, but any conclusion that the standard language should yield the dictionary to the other language is not justified. This other language is, no doubt, more effective and direct in its emotive power, but emotion is not the only thing that needs to be communicated. Linguists would not say that all languages are capable of equal degrees of abstraction. Potentially perhaps they are, but one does not realize abstraction until one has something to abstract.

Last night I went to the ballet — this artificial, highly stylized, remote, supercultural thing. In the audience, since Boston is a small town, I was able to identify about fifty people who live in the central city, and who are not opposed to the Boston Public Library, although they may be opposed to the new addition, and they certainly will be opposed to having any ethnic dances in it. (I am not against ethnic dances either, as genuine ethnic dances. Unlike, say the ritual dances of Arnhem Land, most American versions are desexed and have been revived by someone who wants to restore the Navaho culture or something else that seems good to do.) But I don't see why everyone should have to rise or descend to the level of the ballet, and I don't see, either, why the ballet or the ethnic dance belongs in the library.

We have to grapple with the problem of the new urban poor, and grapple with it hard, if only for reasons of humanity — and probably for reasons of national security and civil peace — long before we start worrying about the untapped and unexploited cultural potentials that may be lying among them. However, this would hardly seem to need the belaboring it got; the real issue is how much of this large social problem must directly engage the efforts of the metropolitan public library and how it should engage these efforts. But even if some or much of it is not the job of the public library, there do remain Mr. Davis' important points that we must understand cultural differences in order to develop the power of lower-class children to abstract and generalize, and that cross culturation depends on the milieu and not on books. These were very important points, which perhaps did need to be repeated as often as they were.

The major difficulty with this conference has been that until quite recently it has not really been a dialogue. With a few distinguished exceptions the social scientists here have been hit-and-run people. They have demonstrated that they know little about libraries and at the moment are only tangentially interested. Mr. Hughes* gave

* Everett Cherington Hughes served as Symposium chairman.

a good example of how much more productive this conference might have been when he spoke briefly on methods of finding out what the facts were instead of what we might take to be the facts. The position of the social scientists was a good deal like the position of the Californian who came to New York and didn't have anything to do. He passed a funeral parlor, and went in to pass the time. It was a testimonial funeral, with everyone rising and saying something about the deceased. At the end the Californian rose — they were all looking at him — and he said, "Well, I didn't have the privilege of knowing the deceased, but I would like to say a few words about California." On the other hand, the position of the librarians reminded me of a scene of Jimmy Durante's, or it may have been Groucho Marx. He was in a rowboat with a lot of people, in the middle of the ocean with no compass. He was saying, "Row, row, row." One of the other men said, "But boss, how do you know we are going in the right direction?" And Durante replied, "Any direction is better than here. Row, row, row."

However, the fact that the social scientists may have overstressed one important urban problem ought not to obscure the fact that they did lay out the background. They referred to the demographic changes and to the growth of the new ethnic minorities in the central cities. I wish they had given more information about the absolute size of these ethnic minorities in what was an absolute definition of the central city, how different this might be from city to city, and what differences, if any, there were in these ethnic minorities. It is a little too easy to describe them all as Negroes and Puerto Ricans.

It was implied — and later denied by Mr. Davis — that some of the present ethnic minorities are different in their motivations from the previous ethnic minorities. Except for the difference that illiterates cannot earn a living very easily now, there might be a question about whether the aspirations of a boy or his mother or father in this minority are really different from those of the Jewish and Italian immigrants of another day. This was not developed, except that Mr. Davis did say — and I think he knows — that the Negro understands that his only real escape from poverty is through education, and so he desires it.

Mr. Salisbury gave the correct and standard description of the political structure of most American balkanized metropoli. There was a good deal of talk about the physical problems of the central city. There was not enough talk about technological change, I think; we touched on it now and again, but we didn't really get into it. There was a good deal of very interesting talk about economics including Mr. Tiebout's highly sophisticated analysis of public finance. (I got an amusing footnote from him: I said, "Well, this is fascinating and undoubtedly correct from the point of view of public finance. But do you really believe it?" He said, "I wasn't talking about the politics of the situation. I was simply talking about public finance.")

It seems to me that seven salient questions became quite clear but were not answered during the conference. The first question is: What is the job of the metropolitan public library? Before one gets to the exact pieces of the job, one must ask, how much effort should the library pay to seduction, how much to encouragement, and how much to service? The problem of how much and what kind of seduction is one every professor has to face every day. When do you stop the corn; or do you ever have to be corny; or what is corn? Are you beginning to sell the wrong thing? There could be so many people seduced into the library that it would be a great success from every point of view except its purposes. How much encouragement after the seduction? This is a much more important question. We have heard about the boy who comes into this somewhat hostile place and finds peace even from the school teacher. How far do we go to scare him out, or what do we do when he does come in? I am still atavistically scared in the Boston Public Library, though everybody is solicitously kind now. So what happens to this hypothetical young man I don't know. He has barely got there anyway and he is about ready to leave before he even gets in. Perhaps there is something to be done here, but the problem, surely, is not to overencourage, to leave him alone and as free as possible. He could easily be too attracted. It is a little more pleasant if not as easy to get into the *Time* or *Life* office than it is to get into a library. How much more should it be? I think this is an important question.

The second question is: How much sharper should the definition of present missions be? Many people here made statements to the effect that there should be priority rankings and that the idea of being all things to all people was no longer very acceptable even to directors of libraries. This wasn't denied very often. I suspect there is agreement on library priorities — educational, informational, recreational, and cultural — though not necessarily in that order. Probably the priorities should not be exactly the same in every metropolis.

The third question, which wasn't discussed enough, is: How much expansion of the mission is needed? This relates to technology. What is the library going to do about computers? What is it going to do about the first powerful invention in communications since Gutenberg, recorded sound — radio, records, television, etc.? It is very possible that important communication with Africans might be accomplished much more quickly and effectively orally than through writing. How about Americans who are not so literate as we like to think? It is hard to learn how to listen; we have been trained to read more easily than we listen. It is also perfectly true, as Richard Meier says, that in some ways the written word is more efficient. But, basically, I feel that libraries have not handled the surveying of recorded sound with enough sophistication. That is only one eligible technology; there are also all the ones that Mr. Meier mentioned.

Fourth, how far should a given metropolitan library system go in specialization of functions by area, and how efficient would it be? For instance, where will decentralization taper off; must there be some kind of library facility every three-quarters of a mile? Is Herbert Gans' statement that libraries serve only those living within one-half to one mile of them even true? I think this is a guess. It may be a good guess, but perhaps one could find out.

Fifth, how much integration of library service and management is desirable and possible in a given area? This is a very important political question.

The sixth question is: Who is going to pay for it and how?

Seventh, what political strategies are possible? We heard something about the various political strategies. There was the question of selling: nobody understands the library. We publish brochure after brochure, usually called "Your Library and Mine." This doesn't influence anyone very much, I think. Most of this is printed; perhaps we should have library commercials on radio and television, such as sponsoring three middle innings of a baseball game. I don't know what it would cost, or how good it would have to be, but there would be a captive audience. The whole matter of selling must be looked at with care to decide how much selling is valuable — and what is being sold.

Another political strategy is wangling. Wangling is a very attractive mechanism which librarians have cultivated already, but may have to cultivate further. Robert Salisbury dealt with this: he called it getting on with the "professional establishment." There are other political questions. Pricing: What are librarians going to charge for anything? We heard quite a little about that. Shall one wait for metropolitan reorganization? I am pretty sure that Mr. Salisbury was right to say that it would be a long wait in the United States.

There is one final thing which wasn't mentioned very much: quasi-independent or supraregional action imposed, let us say, by a state — by a Pennsylvania plan, by a Massachusetts plan. The legislative plans have been discussed. I want to mention one possible line of quasi-independent action. I suppose I will reveal exactly the same defect that everyone else has: that librarians have already tried this twenty times and found that it doesn't work. My own instincts are very much against national statistics and national commissions as guides to local action. Neither M.I.T. nor Harvard nor any one of fifty other great universities would be what they are today if they had waited for a program prepared by a national commission or followed it after it was prepared. No, I think this must be done with very little guidance from a learned commission; it must be done by a learned local group. I am reminded of the great success that the Cooperative Committee on Library Building Plans had for a few years. We were successful for the period when fifteen or sixteen of us were each actually going to build a library in the next two or three years and the work was imminent and real. We came together and argued and thought about every detail, defending our own plans. But we *were* influenced by each other's ideas. After a while this was so good a foundation we wanted to keep it going:

we published a book, and then we were going to make an institution out of the committee and go on forever. We soon found, of course, that those of us who were no longer building buildings, having made our mistakes and being stuck with them, were now interested only in theory. We wanted to make large statements, and the other people didn't care much about that. So the whole thing bogged down. We tried to rejuvenate it by coopting new people who were going to build libraries and by retiring ourselves, but this didn't work either and the thing in the end gracefully died. The vitality of it had been that there was a real problem to be solved by the group involved with the discussion, and that the group was not a lot of other irresponsible people from out of town illuminating all kinds of other problems.

Suppose someone organized a group in Boston composed of one person from the educational television station; two or three university librarians, including one from a weak university library; people from a few key schools, both in the suburbs and in the central city; representatives of a few key libraries of different types from both areas; and a few local social scientists who were familiar with the sociology and politics of the Boston area — men like Robert Wood, who is very familiar indeed with what is going on here (which is more useful to us in Boston than what may have happened in St. Louis). And suppose they had working sessions on a real problem, not all this abstract discussion. They would ask: What is our slum area? Where is it? Where is the library? What is the compass of this population? What can we find out? I would say that after about a week of hard work, trying to structure the problem, one would find that a great deal of information was missing. One really could not do anything without this information, but one would have identified the missing information. The second phase would be to fill the gap by the best available research method, which would mean involving the assistance of social scientists to get answers to these questions by the most reliable current techniques. Then the group would come back together again, perhaps a year or more later, prepare a program, and then negotiate a treaty — a treaty in which the political groups who got excited about it would find a way locally to make some kind of contribution to the total operation. I would even be willing to accept a token contribution from the communities to start. I don't mean a dollar, but something more than could still get by a town meeting. The aim would be partly the program itself but also — more importantly, I think — the voluntary cooperation of some of the separate and different metropolitan constituencies, in a demonstration of how much stronger they are working together. Those who didn't want to cooperate at first could come in later if they wished. This effort would have to include a voluntary community financial participation. Any foundation is a clay pigeon for this kind of deal, but I am sure that seven of you could tell me that it has already been tried.

One thing that perhaps troubled me more than anything else here was a sort of paradox. We say we want to get people into the library. Then the schools, with new programs involving careless use of library sources — not even plotting what the library resources actually are — suddenly dump a lot of students on the libraries. The students tear up the encyclopedias and dirty up the periodicals — generally mess up the library. We ought to be glad they are messing up the books — and then get some more books, but somebody has to pay for them.

The second thing that bothered me was the jurisdictional question between what the school library does and what the public library does. If I were running one of them I would have the same feeling, but I think a lot of time can be lost in having too much of a fight about this. The institution that moves into the void — and the void is there for the school children — will be the successful one. In a simple way one could say that the school budget should pay for it, but to make too much of an issue of this is bad.

I believe the library should do its special job for those who need and want it and that other institutions, such as better settlement houses or youth houses equipped with smaller libraries, should prepare some youngsters to need and want the larger service, just as the schools and the hearths may prepare others. I am sorry if this makes me a Tory. Perhaps I can confirm the Tory position with a quotation from Goethe's *Italian Journey*. He wrote the following about the buildings of Vicenza in his diary for September 19, 1786:

Looking at the noble buildings created by Palladio in this city, and noting how badly they have been defaced already by the filthy habits of men, how most of his projects were far beyond the means of his patrons, how little these precious monuments designed by a superior mind are in accord with the life of the average man, one realizes it is just the same with everything else. One gets small thanks from people when one tries to improve their moral values, to give them a higher conception of themselves and the sense of the truly noble. But if one flatters the "birds" with lies, tells them fairy tales, caters daily to their weaknesses, then one is their man. That's why there is so much bad taste in our age.

Perhaps a branch library belongs in a cultural center as the Germans have placed them in such places as Wolfsburg and Hannover; but the library should not be *the* cultural center.

LEONARD GRUNDT

*AN ANNOTATED BIBLIOGRAPHY OF ITEMS RELATING TO LIBRARY PROBLEMS IN METROPOLITAN AREAS**

The growing interest in the problems affecting library service in metropolitan areas and the efforts made to alleviate them have resulted in an increasing output of literature. No attempt has been made to include in the list of items that follows all of the publications dealing with urban libraries that have been produced recently. This bibliography contains only those materials the compiler believes have a direct bearing upon metropolitan area library problems.

"Access to Education," *Wilson Library Bulletin* 38:335–351 (December 1963).
Two of the four articles included under the heading "Access to Education" deal with the access to public libraries study prepared by International Research Associates; the first article, by a social scientist, is favorable, while the second article, by a public library administrator, is critical. The other two articles center upon meeting needs of culturally deprived children and adults with appropriate reading materials and staff.

"The Access Study; an LJ Forum," *Library Journal* 88:4685–4709 (December 15, 1963).
Brought together here is a symposium of opinion on *Access to Public Libraries,* the report of a research project that was prepared for the Library Administration Division of the American Library Association. Eleven contributors comment, their views ranging all the way from satisfaction with the access study through disappointment to disgust.

* This bibliography in a slightly different form was originally prepared for the Seminar to Study the Problems Affecting Library Service in Metropolitan Areas conducted during 1964 and 1965 at Rutgers — The State University, New Brunswick, New Jersey.

American Library Association. *Student Use of Libraries; an Inquiry into the Needs of Students, Libraries, and the Educational Process.* Chicago, 1964. 212 p.
This volume contains the papers delivered at the conference-within-a-conference held July 16–18, 1963, in Chicago, Illinois. Dealing with all aspects of the student use problem, the conference consisted of the delivery of background papers and commentaries, followed by meetings of study-discussion groups. All types of libraries were included. Recommendations of the study-discussion groups were summarized by Lowell A. Martin.

———. Adult Services Division, Committee on Reading Improvement for Adults. *Service to Adult Illiterates: Guidelines for Librarians.* Chicago, 1964. Unpaged. How public libraries — in metropolitan areas and elsewhere — can serve in the drive to eliminate illiteracy in the United States is described briefly in this brochure.

Asheim, Lester, ed. *New Directions in Public Library Development; Papers Presented Before the Twenty-second Annual Conference of the Graduate Library School of the University of Chicago, June 19–21, 1957.* Chicago, Graduate Library School, University of Chicago, 1957. 104 p. Reprinted from *Library Quarterly* 27:223–326 (October 1957).
Now over seven years old, this volume summarizes the trends in public library development in all regions, including metropolitan areas. The first article, written by Robert D. Leigh, discusses — among other things — metropolitan public library organization and a research library bibliographical network. Other articles discuss finances, population trends, social changes, new approaches to collections and services, and personnel policies.

Berelson, Bernard. *The Library's Public: A Report of the Public Library Inquiry.* New York, Columbia University Press, 1949. 174 p.
A survey and evaluation of characteristics of library users and patterns of library use in American public libraries, this book constructs a unified pattern from individualized research studies. A chapter is devoted to areas for further research.

Brown, Harriett B., and Elinor D. Sinnette. "The School Library Program for Children in a Depressed Area," *ALA Bulletin* 58:643–647 (July–August 1964).
The authors describe services for culturally disadvantaged elementary school students in the Harlem district of New York. A short bibliography of materials for adults and children is appended.

Bryan, James E. "The Christmas Holiday Jam; Student Use of a Metropolitan Public Library," *ALA Bulletin* 55:526–530 (June 1961). The director of the Newark (N.J.) Public Library documents the extent of nonresident use of the central library in this article. More than half of the nearly five thousand users surveyed were nonresidents. The library, however, is maintained by city residents for their own use.

———. "Mutual Responsibility for Mutual Service," *College and Research Libraries* 23:291–294 (July 1962). The president of the American Library Association (at that time) urges all libraries in metropolitan areas to cooperate in serving student needs.

Byam, Milton S. "Brooklyn Public Library's District Library Scheme," *Wilson Library Bulletin* 35:365–367 (January 1961). A plan calling for a network of large district libraries with small neighborhood centers operating as satellites of the district libraries is described. Several districts have already been established in Brooklyn under this plan. Each district library is staffed with professionals to serve all age groups plus nonprofessionals, while each reading center is manned only by nonprofessionals plus a children's librarian. Users have to travel a maximum of twenty minutes by public transportation to reach a district library while a reading center is within easy walking distance of all residents of a neighborhood.

Campbell, Henry C., ed. "Metropolitan Public Library Planning," *Canadian Library* 20:145–156 (January 1964).
The problems involved in planning public library service for metropolitan areas are discussed by the chief librarians of Vancouver, Winnipeg, Toronto, and Montreal. Only Toronto has a metropolitan government and a metropolitan library board; in addition to these, the local governments and library boards remain. The possibility of establishing metropolitan governments and library boards in the other three areas is slim because of complexities that are described.

Carnovsky, Leon, and Howard W. Winger, ed. "The Medium-sized Public Library: Its Status and Future," *Library Quarterly* 33:1–142 (January 1963).
The ten papers presented at the twenty-seventh annual conference of the Graduate School of the University of Chicago, August 8–10, 1962, are included. The medium-sized library — serving a local population of between 25,000 and 150,000 — can be located in a metropolitan area, as either a central city (if its population exceeds 50,000) or a suburb. A variety of topics, including financial support, services, use, buildings, book selections, new technology, and systems, is discussed.

Castagna, Edwin. "Libraries for an Affluent Society with Frayed Edges," *ALA Bulletin* 58:635–638 (July–August 1964).
In his inaugural address as president of the American Library Association, the director of the Enoch Pratt Free Library in Baltimore —

although not referring specifically to metropolitan areas — touches upon the basic problem affecting library service throughout the country: how to provide for the poor more effectively while serving the increasing library needs of the rest of society. A national inventory, or balance sheet, of library needs, which is to be prepared for the 1965 convention of the Association, is discussed.

Coit, Coolidge, and Ed A. Wright. *Planning for Public Library Service in the San Francisco Bay Area.* Berkeley, Public Library Executives of Central California, 1963. 41 p.
As one of their recommendations for solving the library problems of a metropolitan area, the authors of this report propose that the nine counties in the area be grouped into four regions, each of which would have its own system of public libraries. The unusual feature of this document is that it views library planning as a matter of regional concern, rather than as a purely local service problem.

Council of State Governments, Chicago, Illinois. "Interstate Library Compact." Mimeographed release, December, 1962. Various pagings. This release consists of a statement explaining the purpose of the interstate library compact — which is to provide the legal basis for extending cooperative library service across state lines — as well as the text of the proposed compact and a model enabling act. Several metropolitan areas, e.g., New York City, Washington, D.C., and St. Louis, Missouri, include parts of more than one state.

Danton, J. Perriam, ed. *The Climate of Book Selection; Social Influences on School and Public Libraries.* Berkeley, University of California School of Librarianship, 1959. 98 p.
This volume consists of papers presented at a symposium held at the University of California, July 10–12, 1958, as a direct outgrowth of a sociological study of book selection and censorship in California libraries which was conducted by Marjorie Fiske. Selection and retention practices in school and public libraries in metropolitan areas and elsewhere were examined. In addition to Miss Fiske's summary of her research, articles contributed by newspaper columnist Max Lerner, sociologists John W. Albig and Talcott Parsons, political scientists Norton E. Long and Harold D. Lasswell, and educator Ralph W. Tyler are of special value to students of metropolitan area library problems.

Drennan, Henry T. "The Library's Participation in the Attack on Poverty." An unpublished paper prepared for the staff seminar of the Library Services Branch, U.S. Office of Education, April 1, 1964. 17 p.
After providing a description of the economically deprived, the coordinator of public library services for the Library Services Branch discusses the role of all types of libraries in the attack on poverty. Some of the

projects that are being planned and executed — such as the preparation of bibliographies, reading improvement programs, discussion groups, and story hours for underprivileged children — are enumerated. A difficult problem is the recruitment of staff with the ability to establish rapport with lower class people. Public library programs planned for Queens, N. Y., and New Haven, Conn., are described in detail; the librarians of these cities have managed to make their plans seem attractive to the public officials who are concerned with attacking poverty.

———. "Metropolitan Public Libraries in the Sixties," *Library Journal* 89:67–70 (January 1, 1964).
Having established norms for "minimum adequacy" of public libraries based upon the minimum standards promulgated by the American Library Association, the author compared thirty-five metropolitan libraries with the norms for two years, 1960 and 1962. It was found that there was generally an improvement in terms of staff size, collection size, acquisitions, and per capita operating expenditures over the two-year period.

Ennis, Philip H. "Recent Sociological Contributions to Reading Research," *Reading Teacher* 17:577–582 (May 1964).
A review of the literature, this article points out the importance of socioeconomic class upon reading progress. It is indicated that at least in large metropolitan centers, the culture of the school system and teachers is quite likely to be different from the culture of the student; the same applies to libraries in big cities and their potential users. The paucity of research on adult reading and readers is noted.

Estes, Rice. *A Study of Seven Academic Libraries in Brooklyn and their Cooperative Potential.* New York, Council of Higher Educational Institutions in New York City, 1963. 71 p.
Based upon a study of resources, facilities, and use of seven academic libraries in a large city, this report urges cooperative agreements to mitigate shortages in the areas of services, acquisitions, cataloguing, and storage. Recommendations include the establishment of a library council, a study of the feasibility of a regional research library and a storage library, and reciprocal lending privileges.

"Explosion." *Wilson Library Bulletin* 38:43–69, 79 (September 1963).
This issue of the *Wilson Library Bulletin* includes articles concentrating upon the two problems that most affect metropolitan area libraries: (1) increased use by students on all levels and (2) lack of use by the culturally disadvantaged. Activities at the American Library Association's Conference-within-a-conference, which dealt with student use, and at the Dedham symposium on library functions in the changing metropolis, which dealt principally with the urban poor, are described.

The lack of data with regard to library use was emphasized at both meetings.

Fenwick, Sara Innis. "School and Public Library Relationships," *Library Quarterly* 30:63–74 (January 1960).
This article is a report on a study of high school and public library resources in twenty-seven suburban communities around Chicago. Four patterns of suburban library development were detected; the author notes the wide variation in quality and quantity of resources that exists within a metropolitan area.

Frantz, John C. "Public Libraries in Metropolitan Areas," *D.C. Libraries* 33:23–29 (April 1962).
This article summarizes the problems affecting public library service in metropolitan areas. Legislation to extend the Library Services Act to urban areas, and more research and discussion of metropolitan library problems are recommended. (Such legislation was enacted by Congress in 1964.)

Garceau, Oliver. *The Public Library in the Political Process.* New York, Columbia University Press, 1949. 254 p.
A report of the Public Library Inquiry, this volume evaluates the political world of the public library. Of special importance to persons thinking about metropolitan area problems are chapters dealing with the library's political potential and the unit of government for library service.

Garloch, Lorena A., ed. "Urban University Libraries," *Library Trends* 10:449–572 (April 1962).
This issue of *Library Trends* has a direct bearing upon library service in metropolitan areas. The twelve articles cover university library service to nonstudents, student use of off-campus libraries, library cooperation, and future problems, among other topics.

Garrison, Guy. "Nonresident Library Fees in Suburban Chicago," *ALA Bulletin* 56:1013–1017 (December 1962).
Based upon a larger study of nonresident library service in Illinois, this article points out one of the barriers to the provision of adequate library service throughout metropolitan areas. A direct relationship was found between the socioeconomic rank of a municipality and the amount of the nonresident library fee. Fees were established principally to prevent nonresidents from using library service supported by residents and provided free to residents.

Gaunt, Rezia, ed. "Cooperative Practices Among Public Libraries," *PLD Reporter,* No. 5 (November 1956). 70 p.
This publication describes the successful efforts of public librarians in

metropolitan areas and elsewhere to cooperate with one another in the areas of reciprocal borrowers' privileges, interlibrary loans, cooperative book evaluation and selection plans, centralized purchasing of books and supplies, union catalogues, centralized cataloguing, rotation and exchange of materials, cooperative consultant service, planned referrals, cooperative publicity, and duplication of catalogue cards.

Grundt, Leonard. "An Investigation to Determine the Most Efficient Patterns for Providing Adequate Public Library Service to all Residents of a Typical Large City." Unpublished doctoral thesis, Rutgers — The State University, 1964. 340 p.
This study demonstrated that in a large metropolitan city, Boston, Massachusetts, the only public library outlet providing adequate library service to all age groups was the central library. Adequate public library service was defined as the level of service provided by the main libraries in independent cities and towns in Massachusetts serving populations between about 20,000 and 100,000 persons. A system with eight large regional libraries and fifty-two small neighborhood branches was recommended in place of the twenty-six traditional branches found in Boston; the cost of the proposed regional library system was estimated to be far lower than the cost of an adequate traditional system.

Gutheim, Frederick. "A Washington Metropolitan Library," *D.C. Libraries* 32:34–39 (July 1961).
The author, an urban planner, outlines a proposed regional library network for the metropolitan Washington area.

Hajda, Jan. "An American Paradox; People and Books in a Metropolis." Unpublished doctoral thesis, University of Chicago, 1963. 434 p.
Based upon a larger study of the Enoch Pratt Free Library of Baltimore, this dissertation deals with library use and reading. Data came from a large random sample of adults, principally married women, living in the Baltimore metropolitan area. It was found that about 25 per cent of adults have a library card, a slightly larger percentage have used the library within a year, and about 52 per cent have read a book within a year. The amount of formal education was the most important factor determining the adult use of books. A relatively small number of readers accounted for most of the books read; conversely, a large number of readers got to only one or two books a year. This study confirms many of the findings of the Berelson volume on library use.

Hamill, Harold L. "The Metropolitan Area and the Library," *Library Quarterly* 31:13–24 (January 1961).
The city librarian of the Los Angeles Public Library reports that many barriers prevent all residents of metropolitan areas from receiving ade-

quate library service. The relative absence of interlibrary cooperation is noted. The passage of legislation to improve the level of library service through state aid to local libraries is discussed. Research into the problems affecting library service in metropolitan areas is recommended.

———. "Recent Developments in Library Service to Students," *ALA Bulletin* 58:489–496 (June 1964).
The author reviews the events since 1961 in the drive to provide high-quality library service to the increasing numbers of students at all levels.

Harris, Katharine G. "Metropolitan Reference Service: Patterns, Problems, Solutions," *Library Journal* 88:1606–1611 (April 15, 1963).
This article describes the use being made of big city public libraries by residents and nonresidents who seek reference assistance by telephone and in person. The questions of financial support and state aid are discussed.

Haynes Foundation, Los Angeles. *Metropolitan Los Angeles: A Study in Integration.* Vol. 13: *Public Libraries,* by Helen L. Jones, Los Angeles, 1953. 85 p.
This monograph is based upon Ronald M. Ketcham's *Integration of Public Library Services in the Los Angeles Area,* 1942, and *Organization, Administration, and Management of the Los Angeles Public Library,* a 12-volume study prepared by the Los Angeles Bureau of Budget and Efficiency, 1948–1951, with Lowell A. Martin as the chief library consultant. The author, a political scientist, describes the city and county library systems in Los Angeles, intergovernmental relations in library service, and alternatives for integration.

Henne, Frances, and Frances L. Spain. "The School and the Public Library," *Annals of the American Academy of Political and Social Science.* 302:52–59 (November 1955).
Two leading authorities on school librarianship and public librarianship discuss the relationships between schools and public libraries, as well as the responsibilities of school libraries and public libraries for providing service to children, young people, teachers, parents, and other groups. The need for continued cooperation between schools and public libraries in metropolitan areas and elsewhere is stressed.

Hiatt, Peter. "Public Library Branch Services for Adults of Low Education." Unpublished doctoral thesis, Rutgers — The State University, 1962. 246 p. From interviews conducted with users at two branch libraries — one in Cleveland and the other in Baltimore — plus studies of the areas served by the libraries and the libraries themselves, the author found that there was a direct relationship between interest in library use by adults of low education in big city neighborhoods and adaptation of branch library services in these areas. Certain elements of library services were identified as encouraging library use by adults of low education; these elements included accessibility of librarians, good physical layout of branch, and group programs.

Humphry, John A. *Library Cooperation; the Brown University Study of University-School-Community Library Coordination in the State of Rhode Island.* Providence, R.I., Brown University Press, 1963. 213 p. This volume is the result of a comprehensive study of library services in Rhode Island. Recommendations involving all types of libraries — in metropolitan areas and elsewhere — are included. While the libraries are presently independent of each other, the author recommends the establishment of systems and cooperative agreements. State aid is recommended, too.

International Research Associates. *Access to Public Libraries; a Research Project: Prepared for the Library Administration Division, American Library Association.* Chicago, American Library Association, 1963. 160 p.
This study deals with the extent to which the public has access to library resources. Segregation based upon race was found to exist not only in the deep south, but in central cities of northern metropolitan areas as well. The methodology through which segregation in branch libraries of selected cities was measured was seriously questioned by librarians; therefore, the findings of the study relative to branch library segregation were not accepted as valid by the American Library Association. The study also called attention to restrictions on student use, inadequate foreign language materials in libraries, and an inequitable regional distribution of library resources; these findings were received with little criticism.

Joeckel, Carleton B., ed. *Library Extension Problems and Solutions.* Chicago, University of Chicago Press, 1946. 260 p.
This volume contains papers presented before the Library Institute at the University of Chicago, August 21–26, 1944. Of especial interest to students of metropolitan area library problems are Joeckel's paper on library extension today, Lowell Martin's paper on the optimum size of the public library unit, J. W. Merrill's paper on state aid to public libraries, C. H. Chatters' article on state and federal aid to local governments, and Amy Winslow's article on library coordination and consolidation in metropolitan areas.

———, and Leon Carnovsky. *A Metropolitan Library in Action; a Survey of the Chicago Public Library.* Chicago, University of Chicago Press, 1940. 466 p.

A comprehensive study of administrative problems and activities, this book includes a chapter dealing with library relations in the Chicago metropolitan area. This case study has applicability to many metropolitan areas across the country.

———. *The Government of the American Public Library.* Chicago, University of Chicago Press, 1935. 393 p.
In this study, a librarian has described, analyzed, and evaluated the position of the public library in the structure of government in the United States. The types of administrative structures and the relation of the public library to the local political unit of which it is a part have been adequately dealt with. Chapters 9–11 are of special importance to students of metropolitan area problems.

———, ed. *Reaching Readers; Techniques of Extending Library Services.* Berkeley, University of California Press, 1949, 124 p.
This volume contains papers presented at the Library Institute held at the University of California, June 26–27, 1947. Administrators from the fields of medicine, banking, and education, as well as librarianship, present their views regarding the distribution of service outlets. Both urban and rural locations are considered.

Johnson, Florence E. "Private Special Libraries as a Public Resource in Metropolitan Chicago." Unpublished master's thesis, University of Chicago, 1964. 92 p.
The extent to which a sample of private special libraries in metropolitan Chicago render library services to persons not working for the libraries' parent organizations — services for which no compensation is made — is described in this thesis. During a ten-day survey period in 1962, 636 requests from the public were handled at 63 reporting libraries; these private libraries acted as a public resource in the Chicago metropolitan area.

Jones, Milbrey. "Socio-economic Factors in Library Service to Students," *ALA Bulletin* 58:1003–1006 (December 1964).
This article is based upon research which demonstrates that provision for library service (both school and public) to senior high school students varies according to the socioeconomic level of the neighborhood. School and public libraries in eight well-defined districts or neighborhoods in two large cities and four suburban towns were studied. The author recommends that libraries in depressed areas be strengthened.

Kee, S. Janice, ed. "State Aid to Public Libraries," *Library Trends* 9:3–128 (July 1960).
A summary of the history and present trends in state aid to public libraries, both in the United States and abroad, this issue of *Library Trends* points out how the state libraries can help to improve local library service in metropolitan areas and elsewhere.

Leigh, Robert D. *The Public Library in the United States; the General Report of the Public Library Inquiry.* New York, Columbia University Press, 1950. 272 p.
This report is based primarily on the nineteen special studies carried on by the staff of the Public Library Inquiry, which was organized by the Social Science Research Council at the request of the American Library Association. Chapter 4, "Library Units and Structures," is especially important to students of metropolitan problems. More centralized public library service in larger library units is recommended.

Martin, Lowell A. *Library Service in Pennsylvania, Present and Proposed.* Harrisburg, Pennsylvania State Library, 1958. 2 vols.
A comprehensive survey of library service in Pennsylvania, this study recommends the establishment of (1) local libraries with collections of current popular materials for all age groups within fifteen to twenty minutes of all residents; (2) district library centers that could be reached within an hour in each of twenty-seven districts, as a second level of service for readers not adequately served in localities; and (3) four regional resource centers specializing in research materials that could be visited within a day, as a third level of service. The local libraries would be affiliated in systems headed by the district library centers which, in turn, would be satellites of the regional resource centers; at the apex would be the state library.

———. *Students and the Pratt Library: Challenge and Opportunity.* Baltimore, Enoch Pratt Free Library, 1963. 68 p. (Deiches Fund Studies for public library service, No. 1.)
A report dealing with student use of the library, this is the first part of a comprehensive study of central city library services which is now underway in Baltimore. This survey found that although the schools depend upon reading as a significant element in education, adequate provision has not been made for student reading materials, either in the schools or in the public libraries. Public libraries supply almost two-thirds of the library service provided to high school students, both in number of books supplied and number of hours of use; school libraries supply only about one-third of the library needs of their students. Approximately three-fourths of the student readers surveyed were found to prefer the public library to the school library because of (1) better collections, (2) more suitable hours of service, and (3) fewer restrictions and controls.

Molz, Kathleen. "The Public Library: the People's University?" *American Scholar* 34:95–102 (Winter 1964–1965).
The editor of the *Wilson Library Bulletin* critically examines the current functions of the urban public library and concludes that the library tries to serve the student population while it fails to respond to

the needs of the disadvantaged. It is recommended that the large city library seek to motivate use by lower-class minority groups through the provision of materials and services that are suited to their needs and through the employment of staff members who understand their problems and who will reach out to attract them.

Moses, Richard B. "Just Show the Movies — Never Mind the Books!" *ALA Bulletin* 59:58–60 (January 1965).
A young adult librarian at a branch library in Rochester, N.Y., describes how he has been attracting nonreaders to the library with film programs. After some unsuccessful efforts to make the programs book-related, the librarians realized that the young people just wanted to view films — and that film showings represent a legitimate library service; they represent — as books do — a means for communicating information, ideas, and experiences, and therefore they should not "be used only as bribes to do more reading, as inducements to discussion, or as subterfuges for book talks." Traditional library film attitudes will not work with the culturally disadvantaged in metropolitan areas.

Nelson Associates. "Prospects for Library Cooperation in New York City: Planning for More Effective Utilization of Reference and Research Resources," *NYLA Bulletin* 12:1–5 (January–February 1964).
A summary of a larger report, this article indicates the role that New York City libraries might play in the proposed statewide regional reference and research library system. Under the suggested plan, which has not yet been adopted, New York City would be one region. This survey points out the need for increased library services, as well as cooperation and coordination of existing reference and research resources. Studies of users and libraries indicated that students make heavy use of public libraries. Three major proposals are made: (1) that a New York Library Service Authority, a coordinating and planning agency supported by contributions from members, be formed; (2) that a reference library for undergraduates at 42nd Street in Manhattan be established; and (3) that a program for widespread interlibrary use by undergraduates, graduate students, and faculty of higher educational institutions in New York City be instituted.

New York (State) University, Commissioner's Committee on Reference and Research Library Resources. *Report to James E. Allen, Jr., Commissioner of Education. Albany,* 1961. 43 p.
After more than one year of study, the committee sets forth its findings and recommendations for satisfying the specialized needs of college students and researchers. The key proposal is for the establishment of a network of not more than eleven regional reference and research library systems that will work closely together and with a state agency

that is to be formed. The committee proposed that the state assist in the establishment and operation of the state-wide plan by providing to each system an establishment grant of $25,000 and then by providing annually ten dollars for each student enrolled in an institution of higher learning in the state, six dollars of which would go to the region and four dollars to the state agency, and five dollars for each professional person, one dollar of which would go to the region where the person is living and four dollars to the state agency. Public and private reference and research libraries would be involved in the program. This program has not yet been enacted into law by the New York State Legislature.

Peil, Margaret. "Library Use by Low-Income Chicago Families," *Library Quarterly* 33:329–333 (October 1963).
Part of a larger study, this is a report on research conducted among 180 low-income families in the central city of a metropolitan area. One-quarter of the mothers were found to have visited the public library during the year prior to the study. The library use of first-graders was strongly related to their mothers' use, as was the number of books each child owned. Positive relationships were found between (1) educational level and library use and (2) propinquity and library use.

Philadelphia, Free Library. *A Regional Library System for Philadelphia; Contemporary Pattern of Library Service.* Philadelphia, 1957? 16 p.
This brochure presents a plan for providing all residents of Philadelphia with high-quality library service through a network of regional libraries and neighborhood branches in place of the traditional system consisting of neighborhood branches and the main library.

Reed, Thomas H. "The Metropolitan Area: Its Implications for Librarianship," in Louis R. Wilson, ed., *Library Trends: Papers Presented Before the Library Institute at the University of Chicago, August 3–15, 1936.* Chicago, University of Chicago Press, 1937, pp. 45–62.
An eminent authority on cities and municipal government describes metropolitan area problems and proposed solutions. This paper is still timely, although the problems have grown larger and the proposed solutions are more difficult to carry out.

Schick, Frank L., ed. *The Future of Library Service: Demographic Aspects and Implications.* Urbana, Graduate School of Library Science, University of Illinois, 1962. 286 p. Reprinted from *Library Trends* 10:6–286 (July and October 1961).
Drawing upon an analysis of 1960 census data by two demographers, eighteen librarians discuss the implications of changing population trends for their particular types of libraries or activities. The outlook for libraries in metropolitan areas is adequately covered.

Scott, Mel. "Planning for Growth: a Challenge to Librarians," *California Librarian* 22:119–128,135–136 (July 1961).
An urban planner urges librarians to think in terms of large regions. He proposes that library service not be thought of as a local problem, but rather as an area-wide problem. Special reference is made to the San Francisco Bay area of California.

Shaw, Ralph. *Libraries of Metropolitan Toronto: a Study of Library Service Prepared for the Library Trustees' Council of Toronto and District.* Toronto, printed by Grafti-Craft, 1960. 98 p.
A survey by a distinguished librarian, this book principally recommends the establishment of a metropolitan library board for metropolitan Toronto, along with a network of large regional branches to provide specialized services for adults and young adults and small neighborhood branches to provide high-quality children's services and adult lending services. Since a metropolitan government already existed in the metropolitan Toronto area, a metropolitan library board, constituted so as to provide adequate representation of the communities in the area, seemed to be needed to advise the government on steps to be taken to effect equalization of library services to all inhabitants of the metropolitan area.

Stone, C. Walter, ed. "Current Trends in Adult Education," *Library Trends* 8:3–122 (July 1959).
Published five years ago, this issue of *Library Trends* makes little mention of the needs of the urban poor, who are probably more in need of education than the traditional middle-class patrons of the public library. Of interest to students of metropolitan area library problems are chapters dealing with the role of the large public library in adult education, research and evaluation needs, newer adult education methods and techniques, and the education of specialists for the work of library adult education.

"The Student Use Problem," *Wilson Library Bulletin* 37:241–275 (November 1962).
Eight articles by public, college, and school librarians discuss how their libraries cope with the influx of students requiring library services. Improved libraries of all types seem to be required, as well as more cooperation between teachers and librarians. The problem of student use seems to be most severe in the central libraries of metropolitan areas, although the articles deal with libraries of all sizes.

U.S. Advisory Commission on Intergovernmental Relations. *Performance of Urban Functions: Local and Areawide.* Washington, 1963. 281 p. (Its Information Report M-21 rev.)
The focus of this study is on the optimum handling of fifteen typical

urban services, including library service. The report develops a number of economic, administrative, and political criteria which may be useful in evaluating the fifteen functions from the standpoint of the appropriate level of government for providing each of the functions. On the basis of these criteria, the fifteen functions are ranked on a scale ranging from "most local" through "most areawide" in character, with library service falling at about the middle of the scale.

"War on Poverty," *Library Journal* 89:3239–3273, 3376–3389 (September 15, 1964).
This issue of *Library Journal* contains twelve articles dealing with the role of libraries — primarily public libraries — in aiding culturally disadvantaged children and adults living principally in the central cities of metropolitan areas. Emphasis is placed upon the use of funds made available through the Library Services and Construction Act of 1964 and other federal legislation.

"The War on Poverty," *Wilson Library Bulletin* 38:833–854, 866 (June 1964).
This issue of *Wilson Library Bulletin* contains four articles dealing with the culturally deprived: the first outlines the problems, the second urges the use of books to decrease illiteracy and social deprivation, the third reviews federal legislation that is pertinent, and the fourth describes what a small-town high school librarian in Texas did about narrowing the cultural gap in her community. Most of the material applies directly to library service in metropolitan areas.

Wight, Edward A., and Leon Carnovsky. *Library Service in a Suburban Area; a Survey and a Program for Westchester County, New York.* Chicago, American Library Association, 1936. 162 p.
A comprehensive survey of public library service in part of the New York metropolitan area, this classic study includes school library service. Library cooperation is stressed in the recommendations.

"Workshop on Problems of Library Service in Metropolitan Areas," *News Notes of California Libraries* 53:261–314 (July 1958).
In 1958, the California State Library sponsored a workshop dealing with metropolitan area library problems under the direction of Harold L. Hamill. Small groups of librarians discussed problems affecting library service in various areas of California; the New York state plan for aid to local libraries was described; and a political scientist delivered a speech dealing with metropolitan area problems.

INDEX

www.ingramcontent.com/pod-product-compliance
Lightning Source LLC
Chambersburg PA
CBHW020349270326
41926CB00007B/363